P9-DCM-041

Look at them, looking, their eyes meeting the world.

—*William Carlos Williams*

Their Eyes Meeting the World

The Drawings and Paintings of Children

Robert Coles

Edited by Margaret Sartor

Houghton Mifflin Company   *Boston/New York/London*   1992

Copyright © 1992 by Robert Coles

All rights reserved

For information about permission to reproduce
selections from this book, write to Permissions,
Houghton Mifflin Company, 215 Park Avenue South,
New York, New York 10003.

Typesetting by Tseng Information Systems, Inc., Durham, N.C.
Book design by Margaret Sartor

Library of Congress Cataloging-in-Publication Data

Coles, Robert.
    Their eyes meeting the world : the drawings and paintings of
children / Robert Coles ; edited by Margaret Sartor.
        p.   cm.
    ISBN 0-395-61129-6
        1. Children as artists.   2. Children's art.   I. Sartor, Margaret.
    II. Title.
    N351.C65   1992
    155.4 — dc20   92-18677
                                                                 CIP

Printed in the United States of America

HOR   10   9   8   7   6   5   4   3   2   1

To the children who have drawn and painted with my wife, Jane, with me,
with our sons, Bob, Danny, and Mike, during all these years

Preface

For more than thirty years I have been sitting with children in hospitals; clinics; homes; schools; playgrounds; classrooms connected to churches, synagogues, mosques—sitting with boys and girls as they draw or paint. Those drawings and paintings, for me, have amounted to a continual flow of instruction, so much told, though not through wordy insistence—instead, through shapes and forms and colors, mobilized, arranged, presented. Often children don't want to talk very much; often there are barriers of race and class, of language, which separate doctors (or teachers) like me from those we want to get to know; often, even in the midst of the intimacy of psychiatric and psychoanalytic work with boys and girls, a spell of grim, unyielding silence or suspicion or aloofness takes hold—hence the great alternative and opportunity of drawing, painting, together. Anna Freud on the subject—on a certain kind of psychoanalytic technique: "If the child has a reason to become communicative, we will obviously want to know what the reason is—but if the child persists in being uncommunicative, we don't have much of a chance to find our answer! It is then, especially, that playing with children or asking them to draw or paint, may be of great help. A child's drawing can be a child's fantasy, a child's exploration: an account, really, of what's on his mind, or hers. Naturally, we have to know what to do with the information we get. I have 'filed' certain drawings by children [her patients] for weeks, months, even, until the boy or the girl I'm seeing is ready to 'see'—to see what they've shown me, helped *me* to see. It is one of the biggest ironies of this work—that we are made to see, enabled to see, by our patients, even as they lag behind us in seeing what we've learned from them! Once, I sat with a boy, and we looked at a drawing he had done a year earlier—of his father—and he realized how differently he'd come to feel toward his dad than had been the case 'back then.' The boy pointed out to me how stern and angry his father looked in the picture, how grasping and forbidding— whereas the boy had begun to realize that many of those [psychological, moral] qualities were in his mind, rather than in his father. With the drawing as a basis for our talk, he learned a lot about himself—and we stopped talking, so exclusively, as we had been, about his father. 'I realize that *I* am the one seeing you, Miss Freud,' the boy said rather charmingly! Until then, he had spent a lot of our time trying to get me to 'analyze' his parents, especially the father!"

That discussion reminded me of several patients I treated when I worked at the Children's Hospital in Boston—youngsters struggling with fears and anxieties, and not always able to give voice to what troubled them. Often a self-portrait, or a picture drawn of a mother, a father, a brother, a sister, a friend, a teacher, prompted the young artist to realize something, to mention something otherwise inaccessible, or otherwise regarded as a matter not to be put into words. By the same token, as I have described at some length in the five volumes that make up the *Children of Crisis* series, and in *The Moral Life of Children, The Political Life of Children,* and *The Spiritual Life of Children,* it has not been easy for a white physician like me, a New Englander, to get into an easy, relaxed involvement with children who, after all, are not coming to see me in a hospital, or any kind of clinical setting, but, rather, are receiving me in their own homes, or in the school they attend; and so, those times given over to drawing (I do so, right along with the child) have been an enormous help—something that (in retrospect, commonly) the children have come to realize as much as I. One of the girls I first came to know in New Orleans, Ruby, told her mother this, a few weeks after my wife, Jane, and I started visiting her and her family: "I like it when he takes out the crayons, and we draw pictures—then I don't need to talk!" She was a quiet child; she was going through a terrible ordeal, walking by a jeering mob daily, on her way to a "desegregated" elementary school, where she was all alone, the whites having managed to effect and sustain a total boycott; and she was quite unused to having anything to do with white people, especially in her home, where none had ever entered, before we two began arriving as twice-weekly guests.

Similarly with other children: Pueblo and Hopi, also not inclined to talk with "Anglos," or Spanish-speaking children, who, by definition of their linguistic lives, were not prepared to have lengthy exchanges with an English-speaking doctor, no matter his struggles for some fluency in their language. Abroad, as I worked with children in Brazil or Nicaragua or Poland, even though interpreters were always there, the crayons and paintbrushes became a language all their own for us. Sometimes, a particular boy or girl would write a message, attach it to a drawing—or say something to give me a clue as I looked at what had been sketched or painted. Usually, the work was handed over with a smile, and no effort at interpretation—as if the children were saying: there must be *some* reason you've come this long way to sit with us and "make pictures" with us (that is the way children often put it), and so we won't presume to intrude with our interpretations, not when *you* are here, to make them and make them, or so we assume! "Have you got the right answer to my picture?" a boy who lives in a Rio de Janeiro *favella* once asked me—and when I tried to explain that there was no such "right answer," he smiled, and said, "You say that, but it is otherwise." When the interpreter spoke those words to me, I was surprised and wondered if I was getting the right message. "Yes," he said, I most certainly was—and so I had my work cut out: to persuade the child "otherwise," that his picture had "*his* right answer," even as his drawings were certainly telling me a lot about what life had meant to him, what he hoped to do with whatever time he had left.

In the pages that follow I make every effort to connect the reader, the viewer of this book, with the visual life of the children I have come to know. I offer right beside their artistic work a different kind of text than the foregoing one: my observations with respect to their work, or their observations when they were offered (statements made by the boy or girl that were meant to amplify what was attempted on paper), as well as the comments of parents or teachers. Sometimes, I have edited and arranged what I have heard (or thought myself) in such a way that the lyrical side of our efforts to understand one another is highlighted. What matters, finally, for these children, with regard to their efforts at visual representation, may have been said by Ruby, whom I met so long ago in an embattled South: "I hope that if anybody sees my pictures, they'll know I tried hard to do a good job, and I tried hard to show what I saw—what was happening." These pictures do, indeed, show what has been "happening" to a number of young people who have been growing up in the last years of the twentieth century—what can "happen" as the mind takes a look, and proceeds to make a record (sometimes with great aesthetic success) of what has been felt, observed. Some of the pictures have appeared in earlier books of mine; many have never been discussed or presented to readers—and none, of course, has been given the prominence a book such as this affords.

I must start a list of acknowledgements with mention of both Erik H. Erikson and Anna Freud. I have been privileged to know both of them, to have worked closely with both of them, to have shared many of these drawings (and others, too) with both of them. Erikson was himself an artist before he became a child analyst, and Miss Freud had a long-standing interest in the poems children occasionally wrote, and in their "artwork," as she would so often put it. The interpretations those two wise ones offered, as we went through the portfolios of drawings and paintings I carried with me, were often memorable and certainly instructive. Most of all, the encouragement and the sanction given were helpful beyond words. Indeed, I wish I were enough of an artist to be able to express my gratitude visually!

I thank, too, other child psychiatrist supervisors of mine—early advisors and teachers, such as Abraham Fineman, George Gardner, and Veronica Tisza. They, too, gave me enthusiastic nods as I encouraged my young patients to draw or paint and then tried to learn from their efforts. Once again, I thank my wife, Jane, a school-teacher, who has, all along, urged me to "settle gladly," as she used to say it, when we first started doing our fieldwork in the 1960s South, "for the pleasures of silence and the lessons shared by these young artists." I thank, also once again, our three sons, Bob, Dan, and Mike, who have done much of that fieldwork—and worked with many children in various parts of this country and abroad. Their childhood drawings and paintings still adorn the rooms of our house, bring back to us the vitality of their young lives—remind us of the privilege of being their parents, the privilege of seeing them see more and more of the world, its "things," its people, its complex nature. I make mention, too, of my editor John Sterling, who has been a great help in imagining this book, bringing it to reality, and of Margaret Sartor, a wonderfully talented photographer and book designer, whose work with the pictures—helping select and arrange them—has been utterly indispensable. And I mention two good, solid Harvard friends who have helped me so very much with this manuscript, Chris Hollern, a fellow teacher, and Jon Karlen, a student of Chris's and mine. Most of all, of course, there have been those many children. Lord, their patience with me! Lord, their modest and quiet willingness to show and show, and only thereby, tell. They teach so very much to anyone able to look with a bit of wide-eyed wonder—a posture people like me are not rarely apt to forsake for that of the talkative know-it-alls we nervously seek to become during our extended and all too exalted training, and alas, afterward.

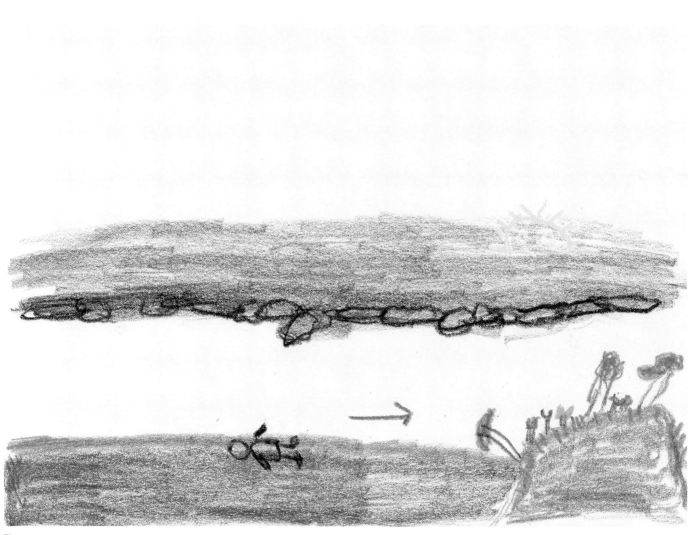

Figure 1

Young Visionaries

During the early 1950s, I was a medical student headed for pediatrics. As an undergraduate, I had met the poet, novelist, and physician William Carlos Williams and had written my thesis on the first two books of his long poem *Paterson,* a lyrically stunning, unnerving examination of America's past and present cultural life. I used to go visit him, talk with him, and, sometimes, accompany him as he met his patients. He was old by then, but he still saw some children—the elderly, wise pediatrician who knew how to calm even the most agitated of youngsters, with a piece of chocolate, a few carefully chosen words, and upon occasion, a box of crayons, a tin of paints, and a brush, some notepaper or drawing paper, objects tucked into his black doctor's bag. It was then, beside him, that I first (as an adult) found myself looking at children's drawings, seeing young people draw with seriousness, even passion. I also saw how much their artistic sensibilities meant to Dr. Williams. He himself was an amateur painter, with a strong visual sensibility and a number of artist friends, Marsden Hartley and Charles Sheeler among them. He was endlessly intrigued by what children could accomplish with crayons or paints, and he believed that all of us, parents and teachers, might learn from what boys and girls have to "say" as they struggle to create images, to present scenes, on paper. "Look at them, looking," he once urged me as we watched some children draw—and then he added, "their eyes meeting the world." He wished that schools, especially, would take the child as artist more seriously: "A youngster drawing is a youngster thinking, a youngster telling you a hell of a lot. When will we know that?" When he asked such questions, combatively, I knew he was struggling with anger and despair and his wish to change the way the young are seen and treated, both at home and at school. "Let them flower as artists," he'd say, "so they can display all their beauty—rather than be cut down to size in drill after drill!"

He knew better, though, than to think that his ideas as a social or educational critic would be realized, at least in his lifetime. As for me, I found his spirit both infectious and frightening. How could one take on the world's smugness and arrogance, its self-satisfied blindness, as he did, and survive? Mostly, I kept his spirit, his ideas, his words, in the back of my mind, as I climbed my way, with great difficulty, up the steep steps of medical training. "Ask your children [the ones I was seeing as I learned to be a pediatrician, then a child psychiatrist] to draw pictures. That way you'll really be told about their lives," Dr. Williams urged. But I was having enough trouble learning about children through listening to a stethoscope, and later, through marching them from one traditional psychiatric question to another.

In 1958, during a child psychiatry residency at the Children's Hospital in Boston, I was asked by a pediatrician friend to talk with a ten-year-old girl who was sick with leukemia, then, most likely, a fatal disease. The child was utterly silent, quite melancholy, whereas most others on that ward, no matter how sick they were, even despite grave pain, somehow managed to do better than this particular patient. As with every consult I did back then on the pediatric wards, I approached the girl's room with a full sense of inadequacy, anxiety, apprehension. What in the world could I possibly do, with mere talk, to be of help to someone so young and with such grim prospects? Still, for some young patients, a conversation or two (or more) had proved useful, gave them a chance to talk about what they were experiencing in the hospital, a chance to give voice to the worries and fears they had, and sometimes, a chance to make requests (for certain privileges, for visitors), which meant a whole lot, even when things seemed bleak indeed.

Minutes into my stay with that girl—whose name, Helen, I still remember—I was aware that this visit was headed nowhere, fast. The girl said not one word. I introduced myself, tried to strike up a conversation with her, and that failing, asked her questions, only to hear nothing from her in reply. She stared at me, then looked away, then reached with both her hands and her eyes for a rather tattered and forlorn doll she had at her side. I was reduced to the repetition of pieties about the hospital, the outside weather, and not least, the purpose of my visit—all to no effect on Helen. Soon enough, of course, I was calling her clinical names to myself: she was "severely depressed"; she was, of course, "mute"; and maybe, I reasoned, not just morose or sullen, but "hostile." Fifteen minutes of such a meeting had me wondering whether to escalate my language further (talk about "hostility"!) and call her "psychotic," or to withdraw with some minimal dignity and self-respect. I had tried to be moderately friendly, but not too chatty or intrusive, and I had failed miserably. Suddenly, I felt a heaviness in my chest, a realization of the girl's grim situation, her sovereign right to feel lousy and sad, and the futility of my kind of presence, my talk, with its own agenda, not entirely free of a sly kind of manipulation. In no time, I'd made my departure—though, unable to surrender (I think that is the right word!), I promised (or was it threatened?) another visit soon.

Hours later, in the early evening, I talked with Dr. Williams on the phone, heard his strongly worded suggestion that I "sit still" with the child and "maybe, do some drawing with her." All well and good for him to say while I rushed about, trying to keep up with what seemed an impossibly demanding schedule. A few days later I was back in Helen's room, now with some crayons and paper. In the interim I had thought long and hard about what (if anything) I ought do. Write a note in the girl's chart, describing her resolute impassivity? Return with a renewed effort at initiating a conversation? Ask for a consult by a more experienced child psychiatrist? The last was my choice, but I was told an interval of several weeks would elapse between the initiation of a request and the visit of the senior attending child psychiatrist, too much time, considering the child's condition. With no high expectations, I decided to "drop by," the phrase lodged in my consciousness, perhaps, as a means of self-protection: if a repeat of the last visit were to take place, I would have less at stake, because my arrival would appear casual, spur of the moment.

This time Helen was largely silent, but she nodded occasionally, spoke a word or two now and then—a minimalist attitude that did not quite rebuff me, but had me, yet again, on my toes. What to do? Well before I arrived, however, I had decided to follow Dr. Williams's advice and suggest to Helen that she draw or paint, and offer to do so myself. We could choose a common subject and each keep busy (and quiet). I had learned to do that—have such drawing or painting sessions—when I had worked a year earlier with children who had contracted polio during one of the last epidemics before the Salk vaccine became commonly available. Sometimes, as Dr. Williams had taught me, children paralyzed by fear as well as the polio virus (their lower limbs, for example, useless) were quite willing to draw pictures, and thereby communicate what they were feeling and thinking, whereas they steadfastly avoided sustained back-and-forth talking.

Five or so minutes into that second meeting with Helen, I was conscious of my right hand gripping a pad of paper, a box of crayons, a tin of paintbrushes. I had to bring them to the attention of this girl—but how? Unwittingly I raised my arm, and thereby put them in her range of vision. Fortunately, she asked what I was doing with "that stuff," and hastily, and with as much earnest conviction as I could manage, I replied with a statement both explanatory and, no doubt, evasively self-serving: I explained that many children have an interest in drawing and painting, hence the crayons, paints and paper I had with me. She was quick to ask for all I had in my hands—a great surprise. Without saying a word, she pulled herself close to the eating table that was attached to her bed and began to use the crayons.

We became acquainted that way, as idiosyncratic a series of meetings as I've ever had anywhere with a child: a series of soundless spells, preceded by the tersest of introductory comments and ended by a scant word or two for our good-byes. She would nod sometimes, as if to say please, or thank you, or yes, and I found myself following her lead with my head. I drew pictures while she did, both to keep myself busy, and to make her feel less on the spot. She often asked to look at my pictures before she let me catch a glimpse of hers, and it soon became obvious to both of us that she was by far the better artist, a conclusion on her part that (I eventually realized) gave her a bit of a boost. Some of her drawings were elaborate and elegant and carefully wrought, but the ones that had the most meaning for her, and for me, were a series of quite blunt pictures, simply drawn, starkly presented. She called them her "river pictures." At first I thought she was simply whiling away time, maybe even keeping me and my possible questions thoroughly at bay. Once she did three versions of a river scene, then told me she was tired not by saying so, but by putting her head back on her pillow and staring at the ceiling. I made a hasty departure. A few days later, she was again up for drawing—and again, she made a river scene. I was perplexed. Only gradually did I begin to realize what I was being told by this girl—who, however, one day explicitly tipped her hand and awakened my mind fully when she asked me, out of nowhere, it seemed, if I'd ever been to the Middle East. "No," I said. "Oh," she said, then asked, "Do you know anyone who has seen the Red Sea?" "No," I said. "Oh," she said again. This time I dared pursue the matter in the psychiatric mode, asking her what she had in mind. I can still hear her matter-of-fact, disarmingly simple response: "I was just wondering if the water was really red."

I replied that I doubted the Red Sea was actually red in appearance. She surprised me with her comment that "maybe it is, though." Her tenacity ought have alerted me to the possibly charged significance of our exchange, itself an event of sorts for us: relatively speaking, the words were flowing, like a river, compared to the usual trickle. Yet silence immediately engulfed us as Helen took another piece of paper and with some considerable energy drew her version of the Red Sea. For the first time she had represented a human figure in her picture. The deep blue of the sea was covered by a layer of red, and straddling the two layers, in a prone position, was the mere outline of a person—head, arms, torso, legs. On one side of the picture an island emerged from the sea, and looming above the water, between the human form and that island, with its trees and grass and flowers, was an arrow pointed in the direction of land. Clouds hovered over the sea and part of the island, but a sun was struggling to appear over the land, so far without complete success (Figure 1).

I tried not to appear too eager to possess that picture! Sometimes Helen offered me what she had drawn—a sweet gesture that spoke sentences, paragraphs: we were becoming attached. Other times she seemed to want to hold on to what she had done, even as (I realized) she was holding on for dear life, enduring one transfusion after another, when that was all, really, in those days, we doctors had to offer. That day she seemed a bit perkier—she'd just finished getting blood—and she offered her picture to me. I smiled gratefully and thanked her. Later, at home, I let my mind wander and wonder—and I began to get a glimmer of what, perhaps, I was meant to understand. I put my sense of things into a brief story: a child is trying to stay afloat and hoping against hope that she is headed for the safety of land. Things look cloudy, but—who knows?—she might see the sun one day. Meanwhile, she is feeling blue, quite blue (despondent and grumpy), though the blood she receives (waves of red to match the waves of the blues she experiences) does offer a measure of respite, if not hope. So, in a moment of guarded optimism (and physical energy enabled by a transfusion), she tells of her low spirits, the river of (blue) melancholy that has taken her from her previous (healthy) life. And she tells of her new life—the sea of red in which she has necessarily been immersed, one bottle of blood after another, and she dares say what she'd like, a deliverance to the land of the healthy, even as she indicates no real conviction that such will be forthcoming.

I had no chance to go over that line of interpretive thinking with Helen. A short time afterward she was even sicker—and she died two months after the visit with her I have just described. We never did, she and I, have any extended, explicit discussion of her difficulties. All through the terrible illness with which she contended so stoically, her tight-lipped watchfulness persisted. She was a downcast child who had no need, it seemed, for tears or statements. Her face told it all, the eyes heavily hooded by a furrowed brow and her mouth firmly locked by pursed lips. Her drawings also told much about a taciturn child, fighting that ultimate terror we all must face, sooner or later, and yet able to evoke with crayons exactly what she was experiencing. Hers was an inarticulate eloquence—that of visual representation. Put differently, she knew how to put into her drawings a mix of the aesthetic, cognitive, and emotional. She knew how to use symbols, make a subtle presentation, draw upon imagery that would provoke others to thought, inspire them to stop and figure out what she had in mind for them to know. Helen was an artist of specific intentionality and considerable narrative skill, and an artist—only much later, after her death, did I know so—who had her own therapeutic gifts. She had figured out why I was there and perhaps found the strength, in an upbeat hour or two still permitted her by a punishing fate, indeed, to minister unto a young doctor trying hard to learn his lessons and much in need of her direction, her hints and clues, her pointers. Even as that arrow had indicated where she would have liked to go, she knew, deep down, rather obviously, how slim her chances were of getting there. Her doctor was at sea, as it were, too, and struggling for *his* island, that place in a healer's life where he feels safely confident of what he can do, and why, and to what (therapeutic) effect.

In her own way, Helen had used that drawing to tell me that she was ready to give me a boost in my training, to educate me in the literal sense of the word: lead me out of my nervously self-doubting ignorance, with its unfortunate veneer of smugness and overwrought talkativeness, the latter squelched by her right off! I had asked boys and girls many times to draw pictures before I met Helen, but I have always regarded my acquaintance with her and her work with crayons as the beginning of my intense interest in the artistic work of children. It was then that I began going over the drawings I'd already accumulated; and in the years that followed, as I worked with Southern children, black and white, going through school desegregation, or with the children of migrant workers, or with Appalachian children, Indian and Eskimo children, I often hearkened back to Helen in my mind, and especially so when talking did not come easily to a child I was trying to get to know, or when the subject matter we were discussing was rather hard for the boy or girl to handle with words. On such occasions, to sit at a table and draw could be a welcome alternative for the child, and for me, too—a chance to be together in a somewhat different way, both of us occupied with crayons or paintbrushes. Then silence was not a threat or an enemy or a source of estrangement, a measure of failure. Rather, it was a sign of our preoccupation with color and forms, with a whole world of visual representation.

No question, when a child of, say, eight or ten sits and draws or paints, he or she has all sorts of opportunities available: a chance to demonstrate artistic skill, aesthetic capacity, imaginative resourcefulness; a chance to make a personal statement, to say something that matters to one's heart and mind and soul; a chance to indicate what one knows—the intellectual savvy that has accrued to a particular mind; a chance to send a signal to someone, whether it be a person like me, sitting nearby, or someone else in the life of the artist. Over the past thirty years I have been constantly impressed by the expressiveness in children's drawings, but also by their pointed connection to the circumstances of the young artist. What is significant in the life of the child comes across again and again in the drawings or paintings that child makes—more so, in my experience, than is the case with much of what passes for (verbal) "communication" or an "interview." Rather obviously, at certain moments the spoken message can be revelatory. But even adults know how to beat around the bush with words—in or out of doctors' offices, and in classrooms, too.

"When I draw, I try with all my might to concentrate, and that's when I do, because nothing is taking my attention away, and I don't have to speak," a Louisiana boy let me know in 1963. It was much easier for him to think about the sensitive matter of race through his drawing and painting than through the spoken word. His parents, segregationists, had taught him to scorn blacks. But he had gone to a school that had finally become desegregated (after a prolonged initial boycott by the white population and much rioting), and he had learned to feel some compassion, even admiration, for the lone black schoolmate in his third-grade class. Initial drawings (Figure 2) of this child as ill-defined, small, featureless (a notorious distraction kept in her own place, under a cloudy sky, by the dramatic placement of a tree whose branches are both bare and twisted) gave way to patient and considerate efforts to represent her fully—even give her a place in the sun, so to speak (Figure 3).

The girl, Ruby, was of course having her own troubles estimating her prospects, both educational and personal. In one picture she showed herself near the school she had, all by herself, desegregated, but under a rain-bearing cloud. The three figures nearby are meant to stand for the mob (some fifty to a hundred people) who regularly harassed and threatened her. This drawing (Figure 4) is full of a child's hopes and fears, and not least, her mind's symbolic life as it sought expression. The flowers, what she hoped for, represent a time of peace, when the mobs disappeared and violence no longer threatened. The blue line over the orange bodies is a way of emphasizing the otherness of a "them," the blue-eyed, heckling strangers. In another drawing, Ruby compared herself unfavorably with a white classmate, also a girl. Ruby's feet are not so well constructed, many of her fingers are missing, her arms are more frail, her ears are missing ("I try not to listen to all the bad things those people say," she once told me, referring to the mob), her hair is less prominent, her mouth is also missing. The sun shines over the white girl, even as a decisive brown line interrupts the grass, which

Figure 2

grows differently on either side of that line: a child's vigorous, detailed assertion of *difference,* of apartness as it gives shape to self-concept, to notions about the world beyond one's own world (Figure 5).

It is not hard, looking at children's drawings or paintings, to see the important influences of personal experience, or the influences of race and class and region and historical moment on a boy's, a girl's, sense of what matters in life—the shaping forces upon the particular world a child calls his or her own. Children in urban ghettos have given representation rather sardonically or mournfully to the impoverished tenement-house reality of their neighborhood existence—a broken-down, desperate version of some of Edward Hopper's scenes of city loneliness, or of John Sloan's "Under the El" presentations of a livelier, more hopeful metropolitan scene. Appalachian children offer the mountains as a guiding presence, a definition of their past, their present, their future, and a means of ascent, not rarely, to God, who surely hovers near such

Figure 3

high places (or so some boys and girls have told me). Indian children out west tend to ignore people in favor of enormous desert landscapes, or heavenly struggles between the forces of light and the forces of darkness. Eskimo children evoke a vast tundra, infinite in dimension and powerful in its impact on any community of people or animals. The children of migrant farm workers show themselves diminutively harnessed to the demands of the growing season, trees and plants looming over their small bodies and (they well know) their future lives. Children from comfortable, privileged backgrounds dote visually on their homes, their acreage, their swimming pools—a world of fun and excitement, and one which, not rarely, they are proud to claim, even to claim vigorously ("There I am, standing [tall] near the pool").

These unself-conscious representations (and self-representations) of boys and girls under ten or twelve show an array of assumptions and expectations already learned and worked into a mind's sense of how things have been and will be. Nationality and

Figure 4

Figure 5

politics also summon children to visual statements, I soon enough learned as I worked in Northern Ireland and South Africa, in Poland and Nicaragua. Protestant children in Belfast eagerly drew the British flag, even as Catholic children drew it, then crossed it out with thick black lines. Afrikaner children were no less anxious than some children of segregationist parents I knew in the early 1960s to demean blacks pictorially—and as well, to indicate a sense of their great and potentially overwhelming number vis-à-vis whites. Black children in Soweto present themselves with the raised fists of protest, and in imaginative flights of fancy envisage themselves lassoing a white, skyscraper world, making it at least partially theirs, even as the toil of their parents and ancestors (in mines, stores, factories) has helped build the capital wealth of that world.

In recent years I have had many occasions to witness the moral and religious and spiritual life of children as it gains entry to their visual world and is given the relative permanence of a drawing, a painting. Anna, a Hungarian girl, offers her sense of the crucifixion—flowers drooped in melancholy, the air electrically charged, a grayness come upon the world (Figure 6). An American boy draws his version of the same event, adds this afterthought: "Jesus had blood pouring out of Him, and He really felt sad and down a while," and so He appears, red and blue (Figure 7). In London, a Pakistani child of devout Islamic faith, yet also very much taken with the blandishments and enticements of a modern Western city whose capitalist materialism has been firmly wedded to its Christian sentiments, draws a self-portrait pointedly, even extravagantly, expressive of the religious and cultural straits he is attempting to navigate: his torso resembles a Christmas tree, while an Islamic moon adorns his head (Figure 8). Here are the boy's comments, spoken in explication of his artwork: "I know we are Moslems. We go to our mosque. We pray to Allah. But this is Christmastime, and people in school are talking of presents, even some of us [Islamic children]. Here [in London], Christmas is for everyone, so maybe it's not bad [for him to be caught up in that holiday], because it's when the stores sell all the good things on the cheap, and you can go get them, and you have the money to pay. My mother says, 'Enjoy their world, but remember your own, and say your prayers when you should!'"

In Israel a boy also encouraged to pray (his parents are orthodox Jews) hearkens back to the Bible, to the beginning of the world, shows night and day being separated from each other by God, Who must have no visual presence, the boy, Allon, reminds my son and me. Still, something in Allon pushes him toward a concrete presentation of the Lord, or at a minimum, His compelling influence, His exertions of vast import.

Figure 6

Figure 7

Figure 8

Allon describes the black circle of sorts in the upper right-hand corner of the picture, perched between darkness and light, this way: "It's God—it's His strength, I mean. He could do that—give us day and give us night. He took that step, and He hoped it would be good for people" (Figure 9). I look at the object again upon hearing this off-the-cuff commentary and think of a giant step, a whirl of creative energy circumscribed by an artist who has taken his own step at rendering things, even as he tries to imagine the unimaginable, describe the indescribable—the Lord's step into our world of place and time, sun and moon and stars.

A Christian girl in Hungary has her own way of taking on such matters. She meditates first on God's "troubles"—wonders aloud how He can possibly pay attention to all the millions of men, women, and children who covet such attention; wonders, too, whether He doesn't, inevitably, overlook people, many people, even as she, the sixth of seven children, has told of her own sense, at times, that her mother has a hard time keeping track of all her sons and daughters, given a serious illness she has. The girl goes further, imagines God trying, trying hard to find peace for himself amid such tensions: "He must close His eyes and try to smile on each and every one of us, but it must be hard, and He must notice some [people], and not [notice] others, and I asked the nun, and she said He sees everyone, and I shouldn't think bad thoughts [about His limitations]." Minutes later she decides to draw a picture (Figure 10) that gave vivid expression to her worries and doubts—and that, maybe, offered a vision of a kind of peace she herself had tried to find occasionally: "I just close my eyes and pray very hard and hope God will see me, pay attention to me, and He'll say, 'I'm going to help you out, and I won't forget you.'"

In Tunisia, a Moslem youth echoes such a sentiment, painstakingly evoking the varied nuances and particularities of a village's life, and in so doing emphasizes the rock-bottom centrality of the mosque in that life (Figure 11). Then, he asks aloud: "I wonder if Allah sees every single thing, or if He sometimes misses something. If you pray to Him, He'll notice—I hope." Meanwhile, he himself pays notice, tries to see all he can, tries to represent for the viewer what he has seen—a visionary side of a youth's life, which he shares with countless others the world over. Each child tries to see, tries to say through the use of crayons and paints what has been seen, tries to give visual expression to a world glimpsed, a world scrutinized and searched for meaning. When I look at such a drawing, when I recall all those pictures I have seen drawn and painted (and discussed), I am reminded, yet again, how earnestly and strenuously children struggle to comprehend the world, seek out its beauties and mysteries and

Figure 9

Figure 10

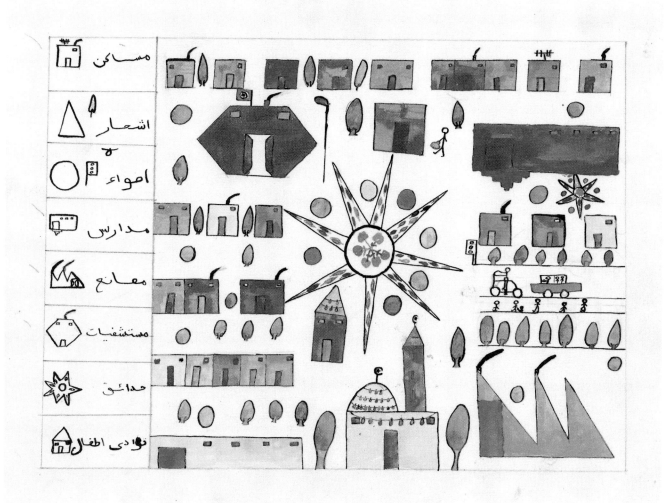

Figure 11

terrors, give them the substance of shape and form, of color, of suggestive or symbolic significance. Hands at work with crayons, pencils, and paintbrushes have responded to minds and hearts at work, trying to define and catalogue and sort and fathom and convey and relate and render: the particular, figurative, expressive efforts of boys and girls as an aspect of something much more—children as budding visionaries, an early version of the essence of what we turn out to be as human beings.

Not that children don't have their own way of saying what I have described in books, and have just put to word, a capacity to reflect upon what they have tried to see, tried to enable others to see. Again and again, children have indicated to me (through words, through a look, a yawn, through a turn of the body) that they have no great interest in talk, and more talk. They eventually find their way to silence in the insistent concentration that accompanies the effort of drawing and painting. Later, when the crayons or paints have been used and set aside, words can return, and with them, a spell of reflection upon what the child as artist had in mind. For instance, Doris, a twelve-year-old girl in the seventh grade of a suburban (almost all white) middle school located fifteen miles outside of Boston, told me: "I never know what I'll be drawing until I start. Even when I pick up the crayons, it's not clear—not clear in my mind—what I'll want to draw. Sometimes I'll just sit there—like I do when I have to write a composition for the English teacher. I guess I'm waiting for something to come into my head so I can begin. Suddenly the words will come; and that's what happens when I'm going to make a picture. Suddenly I'll be picking up a crayon, not just sitting there and looking at the box, and I'll be making lines, or circles, or something." I ask if she knew then what she planned to draw. "Yes, by then, there's something in my mind, that I'm hoping to draw. I might even stop myself for a second, after I know what I'm going to draw—so I can close my eyes and try to picture what I'm trying to do. I'll see a house or a field or an animal (our dog, our pony) and then I'll try to draw what I've just seen, the nearest I can. I'm not really good; I mean, I don't have the 'technique' some kids can show you—they'll draw something and it's really 'true to life.'" Is that her teacher's expression, I wonder? "Our teacher does use that expression, yes. She says the 'closer to life' your picture is, the 'truer to life,' then the better. But my mom disagrees. She says, you should use your imagination, and not sit there, being a 'slave'—she means a slave to what's true to life. Some of our best artists, like Picasso—he didn't just try to copy what he saw. He made things up—I mean, he drew pictures, and they weren't like something you've taken a picture of, using your camera. They're his own reactions, and you look at them, and it's up to you to figure out what you're seeing. There's not just *the* answer!"

Doris is struggling to explain herself and feels at a loss for words, even as she reaches hard for them. She is in the vivid presence of her own, relaxed, artistic intuition—and hesitates to give the analytic observer authority over this side of herself, even as she is learning the sense of command and control that go with words, as they get connected to the world's events. She seems to have found enough security in her own line of thought—its emphasis on others, on Picasso, for instance, rather than herself—to continue for a while. She talks about some pictures by local artists in the town library, which is not far from her home. She remembers the colors in one picture, the shapes in another. She doesn't use the phrase "abstract expressionism," but she makes clear her understanding of the artistic phenomenon—an exploration of territory within the mind and on the canvas, rather than of so-called "objective reality." She is eager to connect her own thoughts and fantasies to such a possible exploration: "I like to mix colors in my drawings and paintings. The [art] teacher tells us to 'go ahead,' and let our minds 'experiment.' So we do. I have some ideas, but I don't always 'follow through,' she [the teacher] says. I was going to paint a field, only the grass wouldn't be green; it would be black and purple, and there would be some yellow at the edge, maybe suggesting a house—when you're far away. It's more a color than a shape, though! I was going to make the sky pink, the way it sometimes is when the sun is rising, or it's falling. I was going to call the picture 'Going Away.' I mean, the sun is going away, and the grass turns dark, and the sky is all aglow for a few seconds, and it's funny, the light, and way away, you see a house, maybe, but it's not a house in your mind, it's a wall, or it's a hill, maybe, or just some different color: all the darkness, the black and the purple, and then the yellow, the house—like the yellow that used to be in the sun earlier in the day, and now it's fallen out of the sky, and it's there at the edge of the field!"

She pauses. Her eyes are wide open and she looks toward the windows of the classroom where we are sitting and talking—as if there, outside the scene she has just conjured up, lies a visible, a palpable, existence. Then, an admission, a confession, almost: "I'm better at imagining what I could paint, than going ahead and doing it." And then a pause, followed by a terse comment that moves us from art to psychology: "Maybe I'm afraid to let my ideas become 'real.'"

She knows to expand upon that comment, does so after only a few seconds of contemplation. "I've thought sometimes I'd like to be an astronaut. I could go way high in the sky, and then I'd look down at the earth, and it would be like a soccer ball, lying still out there, maybe, or a balloon, light as can be, floating slowly, but with no string attached to anything. I've thought of drawing a picture of the earth—when it didn't look the way it does, now: brown for the ground, green for grass. Instead, the earth could be yellow, maybe, like the sun and the moon, or maybe white or pink— I don't know! You should try to *imagine* things—I guess that's what I think—before you sit down with your crayons! But when I do [sit down, crayons in hand] I don't go ahead." I ask her how she proceeded then. "I mean I just try to be like everyone else: I use the same crayons they do, the blue for the sky, and the brown for the earth, and I don't really draw what I pictured I'd draw. I draw what the teacher will like!"

She has been slow to say so. Several questions had to be put to her in order to persuade her to say what she had, in fact, several times already indicated in previous conversations: a tension existed between her occasionally exuberant visual imagination and her conformist sense of reality—the constraints she had learned in school, and too, the assumptions with respect to the worthwhile and the utterly undesirable, that she had also learned. Once Doris made such an analysis concrete, showing me a painting she had done of some spring flowers, along with a note from her teacher, politely but firmly letting the child know that her flowers, painted with such vigorous enthusiasm and assertiveness—a celebration of a spring that had been exceedingly slow in coming—were "far too over-sized." This child had eventually received a lecture on "proportion," on the limits of "exaggeration," and though she had not swallowed and digested the words she heard, she had learned a lesson of sorts: "I wanted to cover my ears while she [the teacher] talked, but I couldn't. Anyway, you can forget what you hear!" But I told her I had bet that she didn't forget. "No, I sure didn't; I *tried* to [forget], I did. But how can you forget something when it's been hurting you? I'd been trying to have some fun with my paintbrush, and she was trying to turn me into a photographer!"

A big smile shone on her face—an unembarrassed show of delight in what had popped into her mind, followed by a few more comments: "I wish I'd thought about it [what had happened] a lot at the time; then, I could have spoken up. I could have told her a painting isn't a photograph, or it doesn't have to be! I don't know if I'd have said that to her, no [she had been asked], but maybe, maybe I'd just have gone ahead and spoken off the top of my head. My mom says you should do that, and she says when you're drawing, it's not a bad idea to let your hand do the thinking sometimes, because if you put too much thought into a picture, it won't turn out to be from *you;* it'll be you remembering what the teacher says, or some book, like that!"

She withdraws, almost right away, from that fantasy of spontaneity, of confrontation: "I guess I should be truthful: I'd never have the nerve to talk back to the teacher—to say what I believe, if it isn't what she's told us. My mom says you have to go along with the people in school, the teachers, and usually they're right. In the art class it's different: you're supposed to 'express' yourself, that's what they tell you. But they have their ideas, and you'd better pay attention, or you'll be 'graded down.' That's what they tell you, what they'll actually do!"

No wonder she had developed an uncanny ability to think about pictures she'd like to draw or paint—only to avoid doing so, even when at home, rather than at school, and even when encouraged to do so by me. Here is one projected depiction that she never realized, despite her detailed introspection: "I had this idea. I'd draw a picture of the sun—it would look like the sun, at first. But I'd put a picture inside the sun. Instead of the sun being just a circle of yellow, like you see most of the time, there would be—well, in my picture, the sun, like it usually looks, but then, there would be something going on inside the sun. I'd put some people there, talking, and maybe some trees, I don't know. We learned in school that the Greeks, for them, the sun was a god, I think, so maybe I'd draw a person, put him in the middle of the sun! I might make the sun wide, really wide, so it isn't just that perfect little yellow circle you see all the time! I might surround the sun with a rainbow—as though the sun didn't cause a rainbow here on earth, but right near itself, after some storm up there."

She denies any interest in astronomy; admits to virtual ignorance of the subject; apologizes for her "funny ideas"; says she "may," however, put them to paper with crayons or paints "someday"; but never does for all the years my wife, Jane, and I came to know her. Indeed, by the time she was thirteen, she was doing no "artwork" in school, had too much else to do. The subject was no longer offered her, and she was, actually, beginning to think and talk like some of the teachers she came to know so well in the eighth grade, the ninth grade: "You can't just sit and draw pictures, or paint—because there's math, and reading, and spelling. You have to be *practical!* My dad says it's nice to look at pictures, but 'they don't make the world go round'!" I ask her what she thought her father meant. "He means that if you're going to go to college, or try to get a good job, you have to get a good education—that's reading and writing and arithmetic. Art—it's like music: you can have it as a hobby, if you want."

But soon enough Doris is having some second thoughts: "If you stop having art classes, then kids won't ever learn to draw—a lot of them. In school, they try to teach you *something,* and the trick is, to keep your own ideas to yourself, if it bothers the teacher [that you have them], and practice drawing when you're home, and there, you can do as you please: draw what you want—and the way you want it. When I'm in my room at home, I will take out my [drawing] pad, and I'll just let loose. I'll make those flowers look the way I want them to, or trees, or a building. I can become an architect, like my mother's cousin: I can design my own buildings! I can just imagine some building, and then, go ahead and draw it! That's big fun! I like to hang the pictures up [in her room], and so, I've got an 'exhibition.' My mom and dad come look. Not my brother: he says no, he doesn't care about art. It's not right that some boys think you're a sissy if you're a boy and you like to draw and paint, or even if you like to go to a museum a lot and look at what they've got there!"

With that subject on the table, Doris is prepared to lament the thrust of an entire culture—and in doing so, call upon discussions she has had with others: "We'll talk, me and my [girl]friends. Lots of boys, even if they can draw really good pictures, they'll pretend like they can't—or they'll almost be a little ashamed! Do you know what I mean? It's as though they don't want someone saying they're an *artist!* It's too bad, because most of the artists, the famous ones, have been men—in the past. (It may change now!) I wonder if those people [the well-known artists of the past] were ashamed of what they did—in the beginning, anyway. Maybe they were, and then they got better and better, and so they got recognition from people, and so they felt different. It's not right, if you've got talent, that you should be ashamed of it because you're a boy!"

She wonders whether, were she a boy, she'd feel any different from the way her brother does. She notes that her mother is the one who loves to go to museums when traveling, or buy art books—though her father has "learned a lot" over the years. Still, when he was a boy, he had no interest in art—and she has to admit, she's not sure she "really likes" the few boys in her school who are skilled and avid artists by her standards or those of her teachers. She is rather quickly anxious to drop this subject of masculinity or femininity as such pertains to art education for the young, yet she is at pains to register a concluding observation, if not a warning: "It's harder on boys— to express themselves when they come to [art] class. I feel a little sorry for them! The teacher doesn't encourage them as much as she does us [the girls]." I suggest that teachers in other schools may respond more positively to artistic boys. "Maybe it's different in other places, but I've talked to my mom, and she says 'generally' it's the same—about boys and art. Maybe by the time I have kids, it'll all be different [in that respect]; my folks say *everything* is changing real fast, and if it's changing for girls [what her parents have told her], then maybe it'll change for boys too—and then we'll have a lot more respect for art classes in school!"

She is a bit surprised by what she has just heard herself say. She looks down at the floor, notices that her shoes aren't as clean as they might be, wipes them with her bare right hand—dust away!—and then tries to expand upon her sardonic cultural comment: "It's still a man's world. (My mom says so, not my dad!) That's why it would be different if 'art' was something boys liked, and they weren't embarrassed, like a lot of them are. Then you'd have more art teachers who are men, and you'd have art as a 'real subject,' not something you do to entertain yourself for a year or two before the 'real serious stuff' starts!"

She draws on phrases she has heard teachers use, of course, her friends too, boys and girls alike. She quite clearly realizes she has touched upon an important subject, one others have also touched upon, yet, she can't continue with the discussion, an acknowledgement she makes by lifting both her arms up above her head! A gesture of surrender. Indeed, rather poignantly and charitably and modestly, she defers to others, to boys: "Maybe you should talk with them; maybe they'll disagree with me; maybe they'll say that I've got it all wrong—that lots of boys like their art classes, and it's wrong to say they don't! I don't think it is wrong, from what I can tell—but it could be that in some other place, in a school I don't know, things are real different. My dad says the French, they're artistic—the men, more so than here, more so than Americans are. In France, an artist is really respected; here, not as much. Maybe that's changing. I know in my [art] class, there's a really good artist, he's got lots of talent, the teacher says, but he blushes when she says that, and I heard he went up to her after class and asked her, please, not to say things like that because he was being called all these names. So she stopped. But she gives him a gold star on his picture [the top grade], and she tells us we should try to learn from him, copy him. I wouldn't say it to her, but I don't like *copying* anyone! I'd rather think of my own idea. That boy does—he draws astronauts and spaceships, and he draws pictures of tornadoes hitting the land. The teacher says girls don't draw pictures like that [on such topics], and I don't know if she's right or wrong. I never thought of doing pictures like that, so maybe she's right."

She then decides to defer to me, to ask me what I have observed. I tell her that I'd hesitate to make a flat-out, unqualified generalization, and that some girls have drawn for me rather violent weather, such as she has just described, and that, yes, they've also drawn pictures of spaceships and those who fly them. As she and I conclude that day's discussion, however, my mind wanders toward a boy I know who lives in Florida who has his own kind of interest in drawing and painting, his own message that he conveys with insistent determination.

I first met Larry when he was eight and in the third grade, and I saw him many times in the ensuing years—until his high school years, when I moved back to Massachusetts, after an eight-year stint in the South. He, too, liked to draw pictures of the sun, and of the plants it enables to grow—but his purpose was different from that of Doris. The son of a prominent landowner who employed hundreds of migrant farm workers to harvest a range of crops, the boy might have easily ignored the plight of those overworked, underpaid men, women, even children, in favor of just about any interest, hobby, or distraction of his choice. But Larry worried about the marginal, vulnerable people whose daily labor, he realized, got translated, ultimately, into his family's wealth. For him, to draw was not only to be imaginative, to render beauty, but to evoke and portray lives, to make a moral statement.

Here he is, at eleven, looking back at a picture done two years earlier (Figure 12): "I've done several like that. Remember?" I certainly did: he'd given them to me. "Each time I wanted to say the same thing: we get our crops because of the sun, and because of the folks who come and pick, two reasons. The sun is 'nice,' my [tennis] coach says, as long as we can go get a cool, cool lemonade after we play. But the sun isn't so nice when it's burning the back of one of our pickers, and he's got the driest mouth you can imagine, and even so, he's got to be glad that sun keeps coming out and beating down on the land, because otherwise, there'd be no work, and that would be too bad [for him]. I like the sun best in the early morning and late in the evening when it's just about to set. You can look at it then, and your eyes don't get hurt. I've heard some [migrant] kids [with whom he occasionally talked] say that the sun is 'friendly' for a half an hour in the early morning and a half an hour in the evening, and then the rest of the time it's your enemy, but they don't stop and think that if the sun wasn't there, they'd have no work to do!"

Even as he pictured, again and again, a sun that virtually touches the land and the people who work it, a large and powerful sun, a dominating sun, he let his mind consider that sun as an aspect of nature, to be represented visually: "I've seen a lot of pictures [done by his classmates in a private elementary school and in Sunday school],

Figure 12

and usually there's a face to it [the sun] and it's smiling. I don't like that; I never put a face on the sun." Why not? I ask. "Why *should* you? Besides, if I *did* put a face on the sun, I'd have it [the face] crying, or the eyes would be closed—because I'm sure if the sun was a person, he'd be sad and he'd feel pretty sorry for what he does to those folks who have to pick our crops!"

Larry seems as if he is about to embark on a polemic, but abruptly stops. He remembers some of the suns he has done, each with its fiery depiction, through long, piercing, penetrating rays, or shorter, fatter, no less noticeable ones, which resemble daggers, or as he once put it, teeth: "I don't think of eyes and a mouth when I think of the sun, but I think of teeth, teeth all around it, because the sun can eat you up if you don't watch out. That's what they [the migrants] will tell you. 'Watch out, Mr. Larry,' they'll tell me, 'or that sun will put the hand on you, and take you away, and you'll be all melted when it's through with you.' I was on my bike the other day, and the crew leader [who procured and managed the migrants for the boy's father] stopped his truck and said to me, 'Better get some protection or old Mr. Sun will grab a hold of you and chew on you until there ain't much left for anyone to see.' I think I was remembering him—what he said—when I was drawing [his picture of a sun that hovered over a field of working field hands, one of a series he did]."

Such moments, connected in a child's thoughts to a pictorial representation of a scene he knows well, serve as a kind of energy—fuel for both an aesthetic and moral imagination that seeks expression. As I sat with that boy, watched him draw or paint, I noticed that he wanted to talk—announce to me (maybe to himself, as well) what he'd heard or seen that had made a strong impression on his young but watchful, attentive mind. He was not loath to embellish his trees or flowers, his homes and schools, his suns and moons and stars—to strive for the striking, the arresting, the surprising—but he was ever on the lookout for an ethical exploration of what was happening (even if he imposed it on nature, notwithstanding his renunciation of the sun's face). Once he filled an evening sky with bright, lively stars, each with a presence of sorts, with a particular field of dominance, and he made clear his editorial position: "I had this idea—to draw the sky and put some stars in it. When I started I wondered if there will ever be a spaceship that can go *that* far, to the stars, not just to the moon. I guess one of these days; and when we get there, we could find some life there, maybe. We think there's only life here, on Earth. But maybe there's other kinds of life, on lots of those stars. Maybe they, up there, think there's no life here, on this planet! Aren't we a star to them! It's all in your point of view, our [Sunday school] teacher says. She told us that you have to think of other people, and not just yourself, and try to see yourself through their eyes, and not just your own—but it's hard. I saw a kid, he drew the sky, and then he filled it up with all these stars, and pretty soon, there wasn't much room between his stars. They were practically touching each other! That's wrong: there's millions, *billions* of miles between the stars. So when you draw them, you should think of that. Would we want someone up there drawing all these dots, and they practically touched each other, and one of them was us, Earth? We'd say, 'Hey, it's not like that—think of us, not just yourself.' You don't go and fill up the sky because it'll look pretty! Well, maybe you do—but I'd rather try and draw things the way they are, and sometimes it's not pretty, what you see, and so you have to try to be fair."

What did he mean by "fair"? Larry's answer was quite forthcoming: "I mean whether it's true—whether you've stopped and tried to figure out what's really going on. If you just sit there and use your crayons to make what you want, and all you're thinking is—well, there's the sky, and I'll stick in a big load of stars there—that's not 'fair' because it's your nice, pretty picture you're thinking of, and not what's going on, up there, in the sky. I guess that's *my* opinion. I know what the teachers say: you should use your imagination, and you can do what you want that way. All right, then why does everyone show the earth to be a ball, but the stars, they're not balls! Maybe there are folks out there, right now, looking out at the sky—it's *their* sky!— and they're looking at this star, Earth, where we live, and it's way far off, and they're saying, 'That's a nice star!' So why don't we draw our planet as a star? I told my friend that, and he said I was just trying to be different; and I was looking for trouble! Well, the way I see it, lots of artists are trying to be 'different,' the really good ones, and from what they [the teachers] tell you, they [these artists] get into trouble, at first, when people look at what they've done, and they say, 'That's no good,' or they say, 'That's a lot of garbage!'"

Teachers' comments, lessons learned at home or in a classroom, get connected not only to a child's vision of the world—his sense of things, his moral and even political viewpoint—but to the vision offered in drawings and paintings. An inclination toward empathy, for instance, affects Larry's landscape: the enormous sun hovers over not only the land, its produce, but the bent backs of field hands. Another child, uninterested in such (human) matters, might have produced an altogether different South Florida landscape, as Larry knew well and was quite willing to mention: "Maybe I shouldn't bother with those people [migrants] when I draw! That's what my cousin [a boy his age, and in his class] says. He says you get distracted that way, and he says I make my suns too big. Maybe he's right. He says I'm trying to make a *point* when I should just be drawing a picture! I guess he's making *his* point, though—about me and my point! You look at his pictures, and everyone's happy. He's got a big smile on his face [in his self-portraits], and the sun, in his picture, has a big smile, and all he shows [in the landscapes he does] are flowers and a few trees. He says I'm missing the flowers in my pictures!"

And so Larry does miss something, though he wants to notice some of his fellow human beings, much to the chagrin of some other fellow human beings, who go under the rubric of his "family members." In his own manner he is struggling first to find out what matters, and then, to highlight his discovery and his conclusion. Crayons for him are instruments of social, economic, and political truth; they are also a means of personal assertion and rebellious independence. He stakes out his own territory by daring to describe in painstaking detail the territory of others. He is a son whose way of looking at and evoking the sun tells a lot about the kind of son he has already become within a mere decade or so—a son who is witness to the sun's authority, a son who does not blind himself to the lives of other sons: "Sunup to sundown, they're picking and loading. Their hands are sure sore." His hands, he reminds me, are not at all sore. But he himself can be "sore"—he can make known his youthful but impassioned concern for others, their burdens and tribulations. The sun lords it over the field hands, even as he, a son, chafes at the heavy hand of a family's power exerted upon them and, yes, upon him. His drawings, again and again, tell that story, psychologically, sociologically, and aesthetically. Crayons and paintbrushes are wielded in response to a family's life (the boy as sharp critic of his own father), and too, in response to a particular social setting (the crops and their harvesters, begging—this artist, at least—to be portrayed). Not that Larry ignores the challenge of shape and form and color—he has his own vivid, compelling style, his own capacity to make a case *well*, to declare both persuasively and winningly what is on his mind. "I love your sun," a girl he likes told him, and he was delighted. She paid no attention to his field-workers, and that lapse, he confessed, didn't bother him at all: "I guess I was glad she thought I was 'good at drawing'—she kept telling me that! I didn't want to get going on 'the migrants'! If you talk about them, people get mad! They say they drink all the time, and they're dirty. But even so, I feel sorry for them! My friends don't, I know it; so I don't talk about it, and I still have my friends."

He knows that talk can lead to arguments, and arguments to isolation, loneliness.

One of the satisfactions art offers him is its silence, its indirection, its suggestive possibilities, which, at the same time, are someone's to take or leave. He is wary already of soapboxes: "If you shout at people, you'll get shouted down!" He'd heard that said by a tough, demanding teacher, and the balance to the statement, the symmetry, had caught his attention. Still, he wanted to register an observation, if not an opinion, and the Florida landscape offered him his chance. If others failed to heed his message, he would not pursue either them or the matter. With some relief he would try to find a measure of empathy for those people too: "My mom tells me you can't just see *one* person's troubles and pay no attention to what's troubling other folks! In our school, everyone is pretty rich—I mean, their folks are! That's why my friends get annoyed with me when I tell them they should remember what Jesus said about the rich people! But He did say it—that we weren't going to get into heaven so easily! Our Sunday school teacher said I shouldn't worry about that, and my friends think I'm 'way off base' when I mention it—so I don't anymore. If they want to look around and think— great! If they don't—that's all right, too!"

This accommodation to a particular social reality figures in Larry's artistic work. He has never chosen to draw or paint a migrant farm worker close up. He is no stranger to carefully wrought self-portraits, or representations of his parents, his friends, his cousins, even a foreman who works for his dad. But migrants are a different matter! As he quite honestly and candidly reminds a listener: "I don't know them, I don't talk with them, I see them—I've played with some [of their] kids, but only a little bit. I'd feel funny saying something about them—I might be wrong. And I guess the same goes for drawing a picture that shows them real big—like the ones you draw of your family or your friends. I'd be afraid I did something wrong. You have to know someone, if you're going to talk about him, or draw his picture!"

In fact, he has sketched people whom he doesn't know well at all; and he did get to know certain migrant children and their parents for a while, when he was five or six and played with a few boys whose parents worked in his father's fields. He could go only so far, he was telling me (telling himself), as he tried to fathom a given social order, hint (and more than hint) at its nature, its structure, make a record of its membership. At some point the person who is documenting the lives of others (as Larry did in his artistic work) stops short of their lives, and in doing so, tells of his own. In a poignant moment (as unforgettable as any I've had in all the years of work I've done) Larry let me know more than I bargained for—more than I expected from him, and more than I knew to ask of myself: "If one of those [migrant] kids was drawing a picture of us—he might not know what to do! I wonder how we'd come out looking! Maybe the kid would show some people standing around, and over them there'd be a bunch of planes, or helicopters, and we'd be in them—keeping our eyes on them! The teacher tells us we shouldn't 'lord it over anyone'—but she means us. If I get in a fight, if I start it, I'm trying to 'lord it over' the guy I'm fighting with. But you can lord it over people and not realize you're doing it! Our maids, they get nervous when I ask for something and they can't find it, and it's not their fault, because I'm the one who lost the thing in the first place, and now I'm telling them they should go and follow my scent until they come up with my baseball glove, or my skates, or my cap. Something like that! The minister told us in church that if Jesus came back again, He could be anybody, anybody in the world—even one of our migrants, I guess, even if they do drink a lot in the bars in Belle Glade! But maybe He had enough of us when He was here that time long ago!"

He has himself had enough of that line of reflection—the enormous barriers that keep us one from the other by virtue of class and race. The artist in him, the moralist in him, wants to put things down, establish a record, even use images, metaphors, to describe with some insight and compassion a certain situation, which (he knows) in certain ways is his—his to see, and his to own, as well, when the time comes for an inheritance to be handed over. The everyday realist in him (we usually become that by the time we're ready for school: a precondition of sorts!) suggests that he stand back, nod to what is, what stretches under the sun: the large manor house in which he lives and the shacks where the migrants live, and his straight back and the already bent backs of the migrant children—backs he renders in drawing after drawing. A child's witness becomes, through crayons, his testimony, a declaration not so much under-stated as carefully stated, with the modesty of a rather special kind of field-worker. He is, after all, in his pictures, leaving one world to attend another—though he hesitates to inflame the local gentry, only dares touch a vulnerable heart or two. Someone who has responsive eyes will linger over those bent backs, the sun scorching them, virtually fingering them, and wonder about things, rather as the boy, Larry, did, for a while, as he accomplished his assignment in a class devoted to art.

If one child can give us hints (perhaps a measure of his privilege), other children can scream at the top of their lungs, or rush at us with their fingers pointing. Fear and hate, those constant bedfellows, can generate plenty of artistic energy, so I learned in the South of the 1960s, when black and white children one day stood apart, under the rule of segregation, and the next day found themselves face to face. Hate can win, in the hated, the compliance of self-hate, even as fear can become infectious, indeed, can be felt deep in the hearts of those who victimize as well as in their victims. Moreover, in the topsy-turvy land of fantasy and nightmare, the hater can become the abject, pitiable giant, even in his own mind, whereas the one scorned and abused rises to smile, to pray—sometimes even to pray for those who rant and rave their enmity. All of that I saw in the pictures of children—the children of Georgia and Louisiana and Mississippi and Alabama, and abroad, the children of Belfast, South Africa, Latin America. The iconography of war, of racial and religious and class conflict, of regional caricature and national pride, have their juvenile genres, as I have already mentioned. But children don't usually sit down and draw that kind of picture at the casual behest of a visitor, a teacher—or solely in response to promptings from within. Usually something is said, something happens, that elicits in them a moment of attention, of reflection, and only then comes the effort of visual representation, presentation. Moreover, children don't draw in a social, a cultural, an historical, vacuum. The Southern children, black or white, who drew pictures for me in 1960, had different assumptions and possibilities than those who sat with me in, say, 1970 or 1980, ready to use crayons or paints. Indeed, younger brothers and sisters of the boys and girls I first met in the civil rights days of the Deep South could be astute critics of their older siblings—and so reminded me of a great danger in work such as mine: one accumulates a body of "data," publishes it in scientific journals, in books, then proceeds to the next project. Readers examine the work as it is written up and call upon it as *fact,* as *research,* to be cited. All the while the world changes, and children respond to what are now new ways of thinking and getting along with others. Yet, all too often, no one is there to record what has taken place: a new everyday order of things translates into new ways of thinking about oneself and others.

It was my good luck to be able to go back again and again to some of the families I first met in 1960, when school desegregation took place in New Orleans. In 1970, a decade after my work began, and several years after I'd published the results in the first volume of *Children of Crisis* (*A Study of Courage and Fear*), I heard black children become quite critical of their predecessors in the elementary schools of New Orleans, the high schools of Atlanta.

A ten-year-old boy, David, whose older sister had braved mobs to initiate school desegregation, and who himself attended a once all-white school, told me this after he'd looked at a sheaf of drawings done by his sister and other New Orleans children: "I wouldn't want to be going to school like they did back then—no way. I wouldn't have been 'nice,' the way she [his sister] was, or the others. I'd have told them [the white people in the mobs] off. I'd have *fought* them if I'd had to, you bet! All those folks, shouting and screaming—they ought to have been arrested. Now they'd be tossed in jail and kept there plenty long! Now it's different. Now black people don't go bowing and scraping at the feet of the whites. Now we can look them right in the eye—we can look down on them as lousy white trash, a lot of them. They shout 'nigger' because they're so low, they can't stand to know how low they are! My dad, he says, 'A white man with hate in his eyes is a white man who doesn't want to see where he's standing—in the gutter!'

"If I was going to draw those folks [in the mob, or the students and teachers at school], I'd show them to be small, real small; and I'd show us black people as *huge!* We *are* huge! I mean, they'll see us, and they get so upset, you'd think we had atom bombs and we were going to throw them! I'd have those white people with crutches; they'd be limping along. The reason is, like our minister says, we're the crutches for the white man! They can't walk on their own—without us! They need us all the time! I don't think I'd like to draw that [picture] though; I don't know how to draw crutches—and if I did, I wouldn't want to draw them! Why be a crutch, somebody's crutch! I'd sooner stay out of school! I'd sooner starve than beg for money from 'them'! You beg, and you're on your way to being a crutch! If I could draw crutches, I'd draw us [black people] walking on top of crutches, and underneath us would be those honky whites, and they'd look pretty small! If there was a white crayon, I'd wrap them all up in a big white sheet—the Klan! You're wise to pay them no attention, all of them. You're wise to build yourself up, and don't let people stand over you, and don't let them get to you—that's the worst, when they get into your head, and they do a job on you that way!"

David "used to draw" but now emphatically doesn't—though he is quite willing to size up what others have done, or will do. Finally, he decides to show me what he can do with crayons. He picks up an orange crayon, sketches a human figure, a man whose shirt he colors red, pants blue, eyes blue, hair yellow. The feet are haphazardly done. The arms are skimpy, far too short for the torso. The hair is disheveled. A cursory gesture with a brown crayon supplies a semblance of ground, but it seems to be falling from under the man, as if an earthquake has splintered it. I am obviously interested in, intrigued by, the picture. The boy notices the attention I am paying and decides to stop any further work with crayons. He starts to crumple the paper. I demur, tell him I'd like to look further at what he's done. He laughs and tells me it's not worth my time to do so. I demur again. He insists: "These are real scumbags! They belong in the nearest garbage pail." I demur once more: "No." He isn't sure what I mean with my one-word answer. I am fighting for the survival of the picture. He wonders whether, by implication or indirection, I am arguing with his judgment upon a white man, and maybe, many white people. I clarify my meaning. He tells me my no will be answered by his yes—he will indeed throw the drawing out, and he does so. I am frustrated, saddened. I want to have a long talk with him about "others," about the distortions that all of us, potentially, are heir to as we struggle with the preconceptions and blind spots that have been handed us as a grim, sad legacy. He is not interested in my historical or psychological comments. "The whites have been kicking on us ever since this country was born. Now they tell us to forget all that, and look up to them, and be glad they're trying to let us into their world. Well, we shouldn't buy their deal. We should say no, thank you! We should create our own world and let them have theirs! That's what I think!"

I am at a loss as to what I might, I ought, say. I say nothing. David starts tearing up the picture he has just drawn. I hear myself saying aloud again, "No." He stops. He tells me he will continue to tear, though he doesn't want to upset me. "Man, you work too hard! You should forget all those [white] folks—their problems!" I am touched that he has, somehow, by implication, acknowledged hearing what I'm trying to say— that to tear up that piece of paper is to surrender to an impulse his people have known all too well, an impulse that ruled so much of the white world, which for so long made short shrift of black people. I say that there are whites and whites, blacks and blacks. I say that we ought talk some more about what's happening right now, the changes for the better—though, yes, there are continuing troubles and injustices. He says he's willing to talk, sure, but he's also tired of thinking about white people. His cousin, seven years older, a real hero to him, says white people, most of them, are "devils" and it's best to "get them out of your mind." He looks at me hard after he says that, tells me I'm one exception, and there are others—his schoolteacher, for instance. "She's fair. She likes us. She told us she's from California. She came here because her husband had to move here. She's not one of these 'dumb crackers.'" He sees me stir, flinch. I ask him if she used that expression. He says yes, then qualifies: "Well, not exactly. She said she wasn't born here, and she didn't grow up here, so she's not got 'prejudice in her bones,' that's what she said." I am upset. I think of some of the white students in that class, who may well come from families deeply Southern, and also, families quite without prejudice. I say what I am thinking. I wonder whether a teacher ought talk as that teacher is reported to have talked. The boy pulls back further: "She didn't actually say those words; she told us she's only been here a couple of years, and so she's not a Southerner."

The boy seems satisfied that his last version of the teacher's remarks is the same as an earlier version. I do not argue the matter. I mouth a piety—that the South, like any other region, has a mix of decent, honorable people, and people who aren't very kind or sensitive to others. He doesn't like what he hears. I try not to blame him. On the contrary, I realize that he has strong opinions, and I ought listen to them, try to understand them, rather than engage him with my all too earnest efforts at even-handedness, a quality of mind it may be a little easier for me (a white adult from the North who has lived a rather protected life) to possess than he. I change the subject, get us talking about black people, their lives, rather than whites. Soon he is ready to draw another picture. I suggest he do a picture of himself that I will add to a large number of self-portraits I've collected. He gets to work: the brown crayon fills the page. A big black man with strong arms and legs, a solid torso, a large face blessed with large eyes, wide open, a substantial nose, a mouth full of big teeth, and a heavy slab of black hair takes form. The man is holding a stick, which the boy eventually reveals to be a rifle: "See the trigger, see the handle, see the sight!" The ground under the man is thick, solid, uncovered by grass. This is a man whose feet are big, well developed; whose hands are also fashioned with care and accuracy. This is a man who could be regarded as a giant, I conclude, and say so when I am asked for a comment. David agrees heartily: "We've all stretched ourselves the last few years. No more being 'niggers'!"

I'm watching him draw, and suddenly he decides he's through. He picks up his second drawing and decides to put it in the back of his spiral notebook. He tells me, a bit gratuitously, I think, that there are still plenty of "niggers" around, though he tries not to have anything to do with them in his neighborhood or at school. I rise to the reference and ask him what a "nigger" is. He smiles. He decides not to answer with words. He tells me he'll draw me one. I am obviously interested. I watch as he gets to work with his brown crayon again. In no time I see a small figure, utterly bent in back, with pencil-thin arms and legs, and no full complement of fingers or toes, and the narrowest slits for eyes, and big ears, a slender mouth. I am startled: this figure reminds me of some of the drawings I've seen years ago, including a few the boy's sister once did. I am about to say something, declare the resemblance, but something the boy says precludes the need for such an observation: "I've seen some of the pictures you used to collect from kids. I've heard my sister talk [about what she and others had done, and about what I had observed with respect to what they had done], and she says now she'd be drawing different [kinds of people], if she was drawing—but she doesn't anymore. In high school, they don't have art classes! We do, but I don't like to give the teacher my drawings."

I realized that he was politely telling me something—that he would be keeping the drawings he had just completed. I tried to dissuade him. I gave him my standard speech about the uses to which I put such drawings in my research. He was unimpressed. He knew of my work—had seen the drawings in one of my books, had seen some of his sister's drawings, which she had long ago, quite willingly, given to me. Still, he was firm, and in his own manner, rather tactful: "It would be all right if you took them, but I like them, and I'd like to show them to my buddies!" I could hardly object. Two weeks later, on another visit, his mother told me David had thrown out those drawings. She had searched in vain for them.

By no means were those the only drawings I have "lost" over these past years. A good number of children don't want to give up their drawings to anyone—and why should they! Tim, a Pueblo boy I knew (when I worked in New Mexico), wouldn't let his mother tape his drawings to the family refrigerator. He wanted them in his bedroom, where he kept them in a drawer. Only once did I ask him for his drawings (I had gotten to know him fairly well), and then only so that I might copy them. He was quite agreeable: "OK, if you'll return them tomorrow." I wasn't quite sure if I could meet that time limit, so I begged for a compromise: a week, no more. In a quiet, matter-of-fact response, he suggested this: "When you know you can get them copied in a day, just ask me again, and you can have them." So much for the grand busyness of my kind, our lists and lists of errands, obligations, tasks, plans. When I had figured out my life enough to know that I could, indeed, manage to get his drawings copied and have them back in his hands within twenty-four hours, he gave them to me, and with considerable generosity of spirit told me graciously, I could have *two* days if I really needed them. With a certain zealous pride (maybe out of an energy that derived from a hard-to-acknowledge sense of frustration and irritation), I made a point of speeding (I got a ticket!) to a copying place, getting the pictures photocopied quickly (I'd called ahead to ensure fast service), and speeding back to the boy's home in one of the pueblos near Albuquerque. He did not seem impressed with my dispatch. A week later, however, Tim's mother told me otherwise: "My son told me, 'The Anglo really learned to run fast.' "

Still, one learns from seeing, even if one cannot, afterward, directly share what has been drawn or painted with others. The black child in Louisiana, David, had reminded me that in ten years a lot can happen in a country, to a region, to a neighborhood, to a family—and so his drawings showed an almost fierce reversal of former attitudes with respect to his own race, with respect to others once so intimidating to youngsters like him, not to mention their parents. He was telling me, without saying so, that what I had once seen was now an aspect of history, so far as he is concerned (and surely that goes for many others). Put differently, he was telling me that the drawings and paintings of children, like so much else that makes up our human discourse, have to be regarded within a larger context that goes under the name of historical change, even as his own personal life, his family's life, supplied a particular energy, as well, for what went through his mind, and eventually, got worked into the pictures he constructed for me, showed me, yet kept from me (and from himself, too, because he did not retain any of them).

The Pueblo boy, Tim, had something else to teach me, which I actually learned from his mother, not him, as he was always too polite to have mentioned what he thought were my short-comings. "My son worries that you are forgetful!" When I heard that, I was quick to reassure her that my memory was intact. So she amplified her concern: "He says you're always looking at his drawings, but then you want to carry them off." After a pause (perhaps to let that last statement sink in), she added: "He can't understand why you need to have the drawings, if you've looked at them! He thinks you must forget what you've seen. He says, 'The Anglo doctor can't remember what I try to show him.' I tell him you probably want to show other doctors what he's done. He says, 'Well, he could tell them.' I've told him it's not the same. But he thinks if you really wanted to, you could draw a picture like he has drawn for your friends. You could copy him!"

This curiosity about my habits (a curiosity that bordered on pity!) had a cultural context. A Native American family, yet again, noticed a certain material possessiveness in an Anglo. That same boy, at another point in our continuing conversation, and specifically without broaching the subject of the drawings he did, let me know this: "With us [the Pueblo people], it's not as important to own things. You should look at what is there—our land. You should look at the sky, and the hills, and the mesa. That's plenty to look at, my grandfather says." The boy's family, parents and grandparents, aunts and uncles, older cousins, had often taught him the permanence of the dedicated stare, when fixed upon the right object—as compared to the transitory quality of mere objects. To look at the natural world of the reservation is to be blessed, graced with an intelligence at work; to glare at what is to be found in stores (including those stationery stores that sell crayons and drawing paper!) is to surrender to a kind of frantic materialism. The boy, of course, never used those words, but he edged close to an evocation of them: "The wind can blow away everything but the sky and the land! Some of the land, yes, that can be lifted away [I had mentioned the possibility], but not *the land*—the land that is always there, to *hold* us." When I heard that last verb, I knew, once more, that I was in New Mexico, on an Indian reservation—the essential meaning of the phrase "Mother Earth" brought to life.

Yet the boy did cling to his drawings, so I wanted to remind him and his parents—as if to let them know that if I couldn't indulge my own "materialism," at least I could specify its existence in others like himself, who were not inclined to boast of such an inclination. Soon enough, though, I would learn that the drawings had "left." What did *that* word mean? It signified a strange mobility, an astonishing independence, for some pieces of paper! The explanation: "We took some of our paper and gave it to the fire [on a winter's day], and it [the paper] was sent out of the house back to our sky." We all know that burnt paper would emit smoke through the chimney. But I felt, and then knew, that this mother's language was telling me something else, that a child's drawings were one small aspect of a complex scene whose rhythms had a certain stark simplicity to them. We Anglos know the circularity of things through our biological studies, yet are less apt to know in the way of the Pueblos. I was in the presence of people whose wisdom was lodged in their bones and was actively lived every day.

In the evenings, perhaps, we do shed whatever parochialism or insularity confines us—and maybe, too, when we are able to let our minds run loose, as much as possible. In dreams, in the rambling thoughts, free associations, of today's analysands, in children's drawings or paintings that are not assigned but come to mind and then are rendered, we who inhabit the various realms of the Western bourgeoisie have our own ways of connecting more or less spontaneously, individually, with our rock-bottom humanity.

Paul Gauguin posed these questions in his 1897 Tahiti triptych: "Where do we come from? What are we? Where are we going?" As an artist, he tried to answer them visually, though he did paint the actual words that are now recognized as the title of the well-known painting. Sometimes, as I have sat with a child who has been wondering what to draw, or who has made a drawing but ponders its title, I can almost feel a certain tension in the air (in the child's mind and in mine, as well) between the possibilities of the visual and the opportunities of language. A picture may seem, for instance, to possess a quite specific subject matter, may have been prompted by a child's interest in one or another topic, or social issue, or question that has been explored at school; and yet, the artist, when interviewed, may mention a good deal that seems utterly unconnected to the message intended, the content represented.

For example, Dicky, who is eleven years old, responds to the daily news of ghetto unrest and to his parents' concerns as affluent suburban whites, but worries about the troubles of city people. He draws a picture of that ghetto, of a black boy ("also ten or eleven") who lives there (Figure 13). At first the white child's comments are explicitly and exclusively sociological: "It's crowded, and you don't have the nice land we do. Maybe a kid growing up there doesn't see much in the way of trees, or flowers, or birds." In that enumeration he touches upon not only ghetto life (its aching absences or deficits) but his own life: his father is a bird watcher; his mother grows flowers, tends them with great care. For a moment, he returns to that other, socially and racially distant world he'd been attempting to describe and thereby understand. He lets me know that he hasn't drawn a house, but rather, a factory. He tells me why he has done so—a compelling mix of explanation and confession: "You see, if the people in the ghetto, the black people, don't find jobs, they'll be in trouble all their lives. So they should [be able to find jobs]. That's a factory, where the kid can go to work, I hope. There shouldn't be discrimination. He should be hired!" I ask Dicky if he knew what the factory workers produced. "I don't know what they make there, no. But maybe, clothes, or something else useful.

"I was going to draw a building where he lived, an apartment house. But I wasn't sure what to do—how they live. I mean, do they live in small houses, or big ones? I think there are lots of apartment houses, only they're not so nice, like the ones you see in the city [a downtown residential district he knows]. If you work a lot, and save your money, you can move to a nicer neighborhood. Maybe he [the boy in the picture] could get a job someplace else, when he's older, and he's had a lot of experience there [in the picture's factory]." I ask if the boy Dicky has drawn already works at the factory. "I don't know if he's working there or not. Maybe he's in school, but also works there part-time."

Figure 13

Minutes later, however, the picture, so lean and forceful in its message (a vulnerable, needy population requires jobs, above all), becomes a child's foil for quite another line of reasoning, no less direct and insistent: "I wouldn't mind if I had something to do when I came home from school, other than the homework those teachers keep throwing at us! I open up my books, and I get tired on the spot! I want to go doze off! My head gets heavier and heavier, so I go have a Coke or a Pepsi! My dad says you have to do your [school]work, and no one likes it, but everyone does it, and I told him, it's not so, because there are some kids, they really like memorizing that stuff, and that's all they seem to do. They're good at it, and it drives me nuts, hearing them talk [in class].

"I told my dad I'd like to try getting a job, maybe, after school, and he said no, out of the question! My mom said I could help her with errands, and she'd pay me, but I would still have to do my homework. My sister doesn't like school, either, but she tries to pretend she does. We talk a lot—and we want to explode sometimes. There are times when I dream of going away someplace and living the way I want to, not [the way] the teachers and our parents [want us to]. I'll be standing in front of our school, and I'm waiting to be picked up [by his mother], and I'll think, This place, it's one big factory, and it's ruling me, and my sister too, and my parents. It's sort of running our family, and we just go along, even if we're fed up, really. Dad says, just because you're mad, and fuming inside, doesn't mean you have to show it. You just keep your cool, and try to get through it!"

As I hear Dicky talk, I think of his picture in a more biographical way, as a representation of him as well as of the black youth the artist's eye has explicitly offered. The factory is not unlike his notion of school—a place where people do what they're told, take orders, and, if they are unhappy about their position, express this unhappiness indirectly. They may be "fuming inside," but they have to keep their "cool": the burning red chest (gut, heart) and head of the boy in the picture is removed from the four smoking chimneys, one, perhaps, for each member of the artist's family. They all are fuming, but they have learned the important lessons of psychological containment, no matter the fires raging within.

But my thoughts suddenly seem rather farfetched, and I try to rid myself of a speculation that is, surely, grounded in my own mind's life rather than the boy's. I am being forcibly clever, picking up on bits and pieces of a child's family life, his remarks, and a picture, in order to construct an ambitious psychological scenario: a family's hidden discontent, if not burning rage, as they get worked into a particular drawing that seems intended to tell of quite another world. Months later, in 1970, as I sit with Anna Freud at Yale and discuss this young artist and his family life and his various drawings, she asks to look again at this particular one. "May I see the drawing of the factory, in the city?"

I oblige immediately, but can't for the life of me figure out why she wants to spend more time looking at a picture I have, by then, regarded as so melancholy and bleak— far less psychologically "interesting" or "revealing" than a host of self-portraits the same boy had done for me. But for Miss Freud, the child psychoanalyst (rather than urban sociologist), that picture was, indeed, quite instructive to behold, as she made clear to me, eventually, in this manner: "Of course he is trying to tell you (tell himself!) what it is like in a ghetto—so far as he can understand what it is like. You tell me it is all guesswork on his part. He has never visited such a neighborhood. But you are forgetting how much children know these days through other channels—*there,* you see my unconscious at work in the choice of that word! They see ghettos on the news; they are brought close to worlds you and I never 'saw' when we were growing up, unless we *did* go and 'see.' Television is both a stimulus to the visual life of children and an obstacle. I mean it furnishes the eyes with a lot of material, but as we all know, it can be a deadening influence, too. There is less and less for the imagination to do. Sometimes, as I listen to children tell me all they see (and see and see and see!) on television, I feel they have been captured by the visual life of the set they watch, and when they are not watching it, they are trying to recover, so they don't daydream as much as children used to. That's my impression, though I can't prove it, I know. The children I see now, or hear about, are excited by what they see, through the courtesy of their television sets, and when I ask them what they see on their own, through firsthand observation, or simply by closing their eyes and making things up, they are far less talkative or excited or anxious to share what they've experienced with me. Sometimes I find myself struggling to learn what *they* have seen on their own, rather than what they have been *shown* by a television program!

"Even though this boy has found out what the ghetto is like, probably from watching television—he shows you that is the case—he is also letting you know something about *his* ghetto, I dare say! Of course, he seems to be talking only about someone else, living a life very different from his own. He tells you that a black child of his age needs a job, needs something concrete to do, something that will build him up and help him find some direction in life, some strength. The boy's arms are stretched out—

you say it is as if he's 'impaled against the building.' True, that is one way of looking at it, but you could also say that the boy is 'open,' wide open to any luck he might find. It *does* look a bit like a prison, I agree, but maybe the boy, the black child, could be saying (or thinking) that he'll do his best—extend himself, both his arms, even if he lacks all his fingers, as you point out, and it's not clear if he even has a full pair of shoes to wear. The left foot seems bare."

I wanted to bring her back, eventually, to the momentary connection she had made between the boy artist, Dicky, and his created ghetto youth. I asked her about the artist's "ghetto" she had mentioned, and she smiled. Then she picked up the drawing once more and looked at it very carefully. She read a transcript of some remarks Dicky had made to me. Next, she returned to the picture and pointed out the failure of the artist to specify a particular building: "There are no walls, no floor. It is as if the building goes on and on, to the left and to the right and (who knows?) downward, too. This is a picture of a rather grim, uninviting 'place,' let's call it that. Lots of windows, each with two dividers, so that there is a cross for each window. And, of course, the boy is a bit like a cross, his arms held out that way. As for the chimneys, they are full of smoke, aren't they! How does the expression go? They are 'belching' their smoke! Why four of them? [I had asked.] I don't know—not for sure! Only the boy can tell us—and he's not here! He's told you that 'factories need lots of chimneys' because of all the exhaust they have to expel, I assume." (I had not pressed the boy to tell me why so many chimneys were necessary—why he'd made such a point with those chimneys.) "I agree, factories do need to 'let out steam,' and so does that boy. He's told you that repeatedly! He's told you, as I understand it, that he's rather unhappy at school. He wishes, quite passionately, that he were in another school [a public one, rather than the private one he attended], a school where he'd have more say over his own education. His parents agree with some of his sentiments, as I understand it, and so does his sister, but they all counsel him to 'go along,' to 'get along,' and he counsels himself along that line—right?" (Right, I answered.)

"Well, I think this picture, among other things, *among other things,* is a child's description of his dissatisfaction with school; his sense that he is caught on a treadmill, an academic one, not the kind the ghetto boy faces. He's letting off some steam. He's saying that everyone in his family feels as he does, but like them, he keeps his feelings thoroughly to himself. Only by a brief indirection are we made privy to his feelings—about a melancholy educational experience! The ghetto boy has to get a job, any kind of a job, or he'll be in big trouble; and this boy has been taught that he'd better *do* his 'job'—stay in that school and welcome its teaching with open arms, or at least, the pretense of open arms."

Miss Freud stopped talking but kept looking at the picture, as if there were further clues she'd not yet noted, or uncovered. She was a far cry from the confident psychoanalytic interpreter. Rather, she was trying to explain not only to me, but to herself, why a child who lives in a rather privileged world (inhabits a beautiful home, goes to a lovely, private, suburban school) draws such a portrait of an imaginary child, notwithstanding the factuality in the artist's possession. After all, she reminded me, I had shown her *other* evocations of the ghetto by white children who lived in affluent neighborhoods—and though the ghetto is, indeed, a place of poverty, of limited or constrained futures, those pictures had skies, had a ground, even a tree or two, a bush or two, sometimes, even, flowers, a playground, a street, with lamps, hydrants, people facing one another, or playing games.

As she made such comparisons, I listened in silence—until, all of a sudden, I remembered something that came to me as do many of our thoughts, it seems, "out of nowhere." The words were: "Schools, those factories of despair." The remark appeared in William Carlos Williams's novel *White Mule*. A wise old pediatrician, a surrogate for the author, is delivering a soliloquy, pointing out how confining and restricting, how disheartening a certain kind of rote learning can be: no questions asked, compliance demanded, exacted. I spoke the phrase, the exclamation, and didn't bother to footnote it for Miss Freud. She smiled broadly, replied with one word: "Exactly." I wasn't sure whether she was affirming me, the unacknowledged student of William Carlos Williams, or herself, the child psychoanalyst with years of experience as an art critic, at once bold and cautious in her interpretations of the work done by young artists.

She was equally responsive, I'd long noticed, to the puzzled and puzzling faces of those with whom she spoke—hence her comment: "For this boy, at this moment in his life, school is not a very promising environment. It is a place where he feels as powerless and hemmed in as the black children do in ghettos, and so he tells you. He sees this situation as almost limitless—years and years. So the picture has no limits, no borders. He has made his own identifications with others who live miles and miles away. You and I may fault him on this. We may think that this is an overworked comparison, and of course, it *is*. There is a huge distance of space (and plenty of ignorance, probably, on his part) that separates the ghetto world from his world, the imaginary boy from the real one. But he's made a point—and others, educators and social critics, have made a similar point. *Anyone* who makes *only* that point is not giving us a full picture, you could say. (You *have* said that—I agree, there are strengths in 'children of crisis'!) But this boy, Dicky, isn't trying to be comprehensive; he is going through a difficult time of his own; he feels angry and down in the dumps; and he wants to indicate to you (he wants to remind anyone who is interested in knowing) that there are certain connections, psychological and even educational, that link children of radically different backgrounds to one another, if all of us would only stop and think about it, about that proposition. He is making a statement, as you did when you said that schools can be 'factories of despair'—*are* so, at least from time to time, and not only in his opinion, but in the opinion of others, who have their say, along with him. He's under only one of those smokestacks; others can find, do find, their similar 'outlets.'"

I am both convinced and (I can tell by my lingering surprise) more than a bit skeptical. The boy is nowhere near us. Anyway, he is several years older at the time of this discussion and, as so often happens, is in quite another mood, so far as his attitude toward school goes. We are not dealing with fact here. We are in the land of conjecture, supposition, imaginative response—the effort of sympathy, the exertion of guesswork, of a speculative foray. I remember, as Miss Freud and I sip coffee, the smoldering resentment this boy directs at an especially demanding teacher, one who taught English and had "fits," Dicky told me, over her students' misspellings. Once he had asked me, "Why does one letter in a word drive a teacher so crazy?" His question, of course, was rhetorical, an anxious, angry *cri de coeur*. Still, to compare such a complaint with the terrible trials of ghetto children was stretching a point, I thought, and said so. Miss Freud gently but firmly wondered aloud (wearing a smile on her serious face) whether I thought *she* was also "stretching a point." I shook my head, as if to say no, but I also blurted out: "Well, I guess both of you!" She did not smile. She gave a good hearty laugh. She continued with the phrase I'd used, taking an implied reprimand seriously. She accepted it and went on to deliver a teacher's response to a student's bewilderment: "I think we both are 'stretching a point'—the boy and me! He's chosen one point of view (out of many possible) of ghetto life, after all! He's chosen to put 'his' black child up against a wall, literally. He's stretched even that point: this is a wall that doesn't look as cheerful as it might! We owe it to certain observers (you included!) our knowledge of the strong side ghetto children have (at least some of them). You have shown me pictures by and of street children that are far more hopeful in their content. Why should a boy who has never stepped foot in a ghetto choose to be so down on its life, its prospects? Yes, he's probably seen documentaries on television [I had reminded her of that possibility, reminded her of her own earlier reminder to me]. But those documentaries usually present a mixture of moods and attitudes. Often they are criticized for not being true to the facts, for being too upbeat. That's what I have heard from people who are in politics, working on the side of the poor. Even if this boy saw an especially gloomy television program, I'm still left to wonder why he took it so much to heart. I am suggesting that he did that because in some way that [ghetto] child's experience, as he drew it, said something about his own.

"When children draw pictures (any kind, no matter the subject), they are putting themselves forth—[that is] pure common sense, I realize. They are telling us what they see, what they want to see, what they hope someday to see, and very important, what they hope *we* will see about them, or sometimes, what they may hope we don't see, while at the same time what they dare hope we do, after all, see. The more you think of all this, the more complicated it becomes, I realize! A drawing is its own Rorschach test! We impose our thinking and feeling on those [Rorschach] cards; and by the same token, we impose our thinking and feeling with crayons on paper. You are right, there is 'objective reality,' making its demands on our skill. [I had mentioned that variable.] But there are many ways of presenting that 'objective reality'! This boy, actually, hasn't been all that faithful to 'objective reality'! He has let his scene, his fantasy, his interpretation, hang in a limbo, you could say—between the ground and the sky! The more I look at that [ghetto] boy, the more I see him, in that picture, as a door, almost, to the building, a point of entry, standing in lieu of a door, I should say! He will tell us what the artist thinks—not only about the ghetto! But I can see that I am not having success at persuading you!"

She was having some success, but I was (maybe still am) reluctant to feel authoritative about anyone's "interpretation" of a drawing or painting, be it a child's, or an adult artist's. I appreciated the possible correctness of her psychoanalytic appraisal of the boy himself, at least as she had heard of him through me. But his drawing told me, I kept thinking, of one boy's brave leap toward another's life—without, necessarily, any baggage of his own. Maybe, I kept thinking, those four black chimneys, with their sooty expulsions, were nothing more than a child's way of saying: "It is an exceedingly hard life over there, and I must find (I have found!) a symbolic way of saying as much." Why go any further? In the end, as Miss Freud and I bantered a bit more (and as she realized I was being compliantly accepting of her angle of vision but not entirely willing to see things as she did), she rather charmingly and winningly offered a truce, if not a resolution! "Perhaps we can agree that your young artist, Dicky, has given us a provocative young man. The picture makes us stop and wonder: a good, strong one on that account!" I nodded more decisively than had been the case earlier, and we went on to other matters.

Months later, as I was going over a host of old notes and transcripts, looking for self-descriptions of black children, and descriptions of them by others who were at school with them in "integrated" classrooms, I came across pages of comments by Dicky and his classmates. They had taken a field trip into Boston, had actually seen a ghetto, albeit through the windows of a school bus on its way to a museum located at the edge of a public housing project. Dicky, characteristically, was self-critical as he talked of that trip, but also quite self-revealing: "I feel ashamed. We were 'slumming,' my dad said [afterward, when the family talked about the trip]. The driver said he sure was glad he didn't live there! It was a long ride, and the driver got lost for a while, and it was bumpy on the bus, and some kids got car-sick, and I was almost one of them. I could feel my stomach starting to get queasy just as we got there, and so I was sure glad to get off that bus! All the time, in the museum, we wanted to get out of there, but we couldn't. They kept telling us things—and telling us to be quiet and listen! A couple of times, I thought of those [ghetto] kids I saw playing catch in the street. I wished I was out there, doing that! They should have us go and meet some of those kids, and we could play and get to know each other, and that would be a good idea. I was almost going to say something to our teacher [who went on the trip], but I thought he might not like the idea. Then, on the way home, I heard kids saying what a 'lousy neighborhood' we were going through and how 'bad' it must be, to live there— for kids, like us. I spoke up. I said, 'They didn't seem so unhappy this morning, when we were driving through!' No one said anything. Maybe they hadn't even seen the kids out there, playing and kidding and laughing. Pretty soon everyone was talking about other stuff, but I kept thinking of those kids I'd seen, and I told my folks about them, and they said we should have some of those kids at our school, to go there. But I don't know if they'd want to come all the way out to our town. Besides, my dad is always criticizing our school—and I do, a lot, so why should we wish it on those kids! I know [I had suggested the obvious educational benefits], but still, maybe those kids would be happier where they are. Maybe if they came out here, they'd want to leave after they met some people—or they'd get angry a lot but keep quiet and not tell [others] how they feel!"

That last remark evoked memories of Miss Freud looking at his drawing, wondering about some of *his* anger directed at his school. I was, yet again, reminded that a child can use any drawing in a number of ways: to tell a story; convey information; indicate something that is happening; connect the foregoing to his or her life, to a range of ideas or attitudes or concerns or worries that press for expression, even as they may be denied that expression, at least directly. The picture, then, like much of what we say and write, is a compromise of sorts—the mind seeking to convey what it feels, while at the same time taking its constant measure of things, lest it run into a good deal of doubt, if not antagonism, from others. Dicky on the bus was similarly preoccupied: how much should he say so that he would be not only heard, but understood, heeded? He spoke some words, used the response his schoolmates might make as a litmus test, heard nothing, pulled back into his own musing life. Whereas others on the bus felt sorry for the ghetto inhabitants, he was inclined to worry about his own world's inhabitants, some right near him on the bus. His picture, I began to realize, may well have been an earlier version of such a leap back and forth, a boy straddling two distinctly different neighborhoods, and willing to try to comprehend one from the point of view of the other. Yet, interestingly, the black boy in the picture Miss Freud and I had examined together is deprived of a view, despite all the windows behind him, even as his artist-creator, Dicky, felt himself to be in a similar bind: "'Try to have a long-range look,' Mom and Dad say, but most of the time I'm trying to get my spelling 'up to snuff' [the teacher's expression] in class, or listening to someone brag about how much dough his dad made last year."

Such a remark prompts mention of another aspect of children's art: the traditional function of poster art and the traditional prerogative of such serious and renowned and diverse artists as Goya, Kollwitz, Picasso, Hopper, Remington—social comment, rhetorical assertion. Politics, we are often told, can spoil art, turn it into special pleading, or propaganda, or all too unqualified posturing. Still, an artist capable of indirection can avoid such hazards, give his or her picture an inspired, summoning subtlety which, nevertheless, achieves a desired effect with great power and persuasive intensity. In its own unpretentious way, Dicky's drawing is in that tradition. One can argue that the boy in the picture, with his back to the factory, has his arms stretched in either suffering or welcoming. He may be saying, "Here I am, and here it is—a world you the viewer most likely comprehend as little as the artist." Yet look at what that artist, paradoxically, *did* understand! Once, when I showed that drawing to a black child of twelve in a Boston ghetto, a boy named Carl, I heard this response: "The kid, he's fed up, but I can see that he's tough. He looks to me like he could outrun anyone—a real cool cat, with those thin legs! He's up on his toes, don't you see! [I did, right then, see the boy's right foot in that new way, on his toes!] He's ready for any comers! Just let them try and fool with him! He could have his 'protection' in that black leather jacket, inside it, out of sight! His right hand—it seems to end in a point! I was wondering if the guy was holding a knife. Maybe someone is around the corner, or is driving by, and he could stop, he could mean trouble, so you've got to keep your eyes glued on the street. You turn your back, you gaze through a window, and you could be done for real quick, before you even know it."

As I listened to such taped remarks later, with the picture before me, I wondered what Miss Freud would make of them, though by then, 1984, she had been dead for two years. She would no doubt have wanted to know a lot more about Carl, and she surely would have said again what I'd heard her state once, as together we pored over a stack of children's artistic productions (pencil sketches, drawings done with crayons or felt-tip markers, conventional realistic paintings and not a few that might qualify as the abstract expressionist kind): "We are what we see." She knew better than to let an aphorism like that stand on its own, unmodified. But she also knew how earnestly and readily and often heartily we pour ourselves into what we see, what we notice in the world, or with crayons or paints, ask others to notice.

Often I have sat with groups of children as they look at one another's artistic work. Indeed, for several years I have taught a fourth-grade class and asked the boys and girls to comment not only on their own work, but (through the use of slides) some of the work of well-known artists: Rembrandt, Renoir, Rouault, Klee, Munch, Hopper, Picasso, Van Gogh, Gauguin—especially Hopper, whose particular kind of American realism, with its striking, sometimes haunting light and shadows, has summoned many a personal response from those young viewers. Every week in an English class, I asked the children to write about what they had seen. I started doing so out of desperation. The children lived in a ghetto, and at eight and nine were already, by and large, vastly uninterested in school, and assertively, even truculently, determined to do as little as possible while there. "I have nothing to say" was a common refrain, both declared by students in class and even written on tests. Some of the children even competed for the lowest grades possible, to the point that I was almost always frustrated and sometimes teetering between anger and despair. Finally, I surrendered to the claim, the complaint, the *boast* of the children, that they had little or nothing to tell, whether in classroom discussions or in the compositions I assigned. Instead, I asked them to draw pictures—of themselves, of others, of any scene or subject they wished; and I also showed them the pictures, without, at first, telling them about who the artists were, or what they were intending to do as they worked on their canvases.

Hopper's well-known *Nighthawks* elicited immediate attention, silent contemplation, enormous curiosity. The room had never been so quiet—in hushed awe, almost, followed by a flood of comments, many of them frankly personal. The children talked of their visits to restaurants, cafeterias; they told of family members who worked in them; they speculated on the lives of the figures Hopper painted and connected those lives to their own. One girl, whose mother worked "the midnight to morning" shift at Dunkin' Donuts, held the class spellbound by her account of who stopped, at those hours, to be served. That same girl had never spoken a word before in class. She had written very little, too, but now wrote a long, arresting, touching composition, titled "People My Mother Feeds at Midnight." She ended her paper by designating those people as "Dunkin' Donuts Nighthawks." There were plenty of spelling mistakes and not a few errors of grammar. But the essay flowed along swiftly with vivid, detailed descriptions, along with shrewd portrayals of character, and even some unforgettable dialogue. Others also wrote strikingly original and poignant compositions. The activity was a big success, which I kept remembering as my "Nighthawk Day." But with all due respect to Hopper, other artists were also successful in exciting the children, prompting them to pay close attention, to speak thoughtfully in class, to write with care and sometimes great passion—artists who were the same age as these children were.

I stumbled upon the idea of offering children the work of their age-mates. I had a stack of slides to show the children—well-known paintings from various museums—but interspersed, by accident, were slides of drawings done for me by boys and girls when I lived and worked in New Mexico during the 1970s. As I started the slide machine going and tried to catch my bearings, one of the New Mexico drawings (Figure 14) suddenly appeared on the screen. The children rose noisily, ardently, to the moment. I moved on, muttering that I'd made a mistake, that my various piles of slides had gotten mixed up. But they would have no part of my plans, my explanation. They wanted to see the picture again. They wanted to know who did it and who had been portrayed. They also wanted to answer these questions themselves and started doing so before I had a chance to say much. I did manage to let them know that the picture was done "a few years ago," drawn by a girl who was approximately

Figure 14

their age, nine at the time, and that she lived in New Mexico. The class exploded with comments, exchanges of impressions, discussion, argument. In fact, the artist, a Pueblo child, Rose, had drawn an Indian man who worked for the Bureau of Indian Affairs. But for these urban children, living in a poor Greater Boston neighborhood, the portrait had an eerily intimate significance that struck me, at the time, as perplexing. The children went back and forth with their statements, their agreements and disagreements. The person in the picture was black, was white; was a man, was a woman; was sick, was sleepy, was using drugs, was upset, was tired, was jobless, was going to work, was coming home from work; was young, was old. In a sense, this figure became for each child an extension of his or her life, and for us, listening, an introduction to it.

Many of the youngsters made mention of the person's eyes and, as well, the ears. A girl who called the figure "an old man" said he'd been listening to so much all his life that he'd grown big ears, and he'd seen so much that he'd grown tired of seeing, so he closed his eyes. She was "sure," by the way, that he was black, and she told us why: "I know people like that, because it's my grandma and my granddaddy. They're the ones who are raising me. My [grand]daddy, he's over fifty. He's working as a guard, and he cleans offices. He listens to people all day, and they say things, and they don't think he can hear. They forget he's got ears, like they do. He lets them think he's deaf, and he says he half closes his eyes, so people think he doesn't see anything—but he does. He looks at what's on the desks when he's cleaning, and he puts it together with what they say, and that way he knows what's going on.

"If you're black, and you're cleaning up after people, they think you're like an ashtray, or a wastepaper basket: you pick up what they throw away! That guy [in the picture] is listening; he's bent his head a little, and he's hearing people talk, and he knows what they mean. But they don't give him any credit; they talk as though he's no one, and he gets a kick out of it, knowing he's been fooling them! He looks happy to me. I think there's a smile in his mind, even if he's not wearing it on his face!"

Others obviously saw a different picture. One of the three white children in the class, a nine-year-old boy, insisted that the man was dozing, even though standing: "He's asleep! He might be on drugs, maybe, or he might drink too much. He's in a [small neighborhood] park, but it's in the city. There's only a small lawn near him. He might end up sleeping on a bench there, if he doesn't get arrested for hanging around and making a mess. I see people like him on my way to school. They've been sleeping on benches, maybe, or the gutters, and they look as though they'll never really wake up and be normal! The police come sometimes and clear them out! Otherwise, no one could use that park."

A black girl is convinced, however, that the picture is one of a "tired" black woman who has many children and tries hard to stand by all of them: "She's been working, and she's on her way home, and she's about to go to sleep, so she's nodding, but she has to keep going because she needs to get home fast and cook supper for everyone. She's probably dreaming of a long weekend she might get one of these days, when she could sleep all she wants and someone could come and cook for us, maybe her sister. The trouble is her sister, she's real sick, she's in the hospital, because her heart doesn't work right."

When that description ends, silence holds the class for ten seconds or so, a long time. I decide to ask the girl, "Do you know anyone like the person you've just told us about?" Immediately, and with no shyness or embarrassment, the girl says, "Yes, my momma—she's my momma's momma, but my momma died a long time ago, and so she's our momma." The girl now adds some details to her story, realizing she has even more to tell us: "My momma took the wrong medicine, and she just died." A further silence. Then I see a few students whispering, and by their all too savvy, knowing expressions, I surmise what they are saying, even as I myself thought likewise: a drug overdose. Later, I would find out that they (and I) had guessed correctly. The girl finishes her story by saying, poignantly, that "maybe she [the person pictured] is remembering someone, while she's walking home, or she's wishing someone was there with her, walking." We sit still and silent for another ten or fifteen seconds. The children don't even fidget. I start wondering which picture to show next—a picture done by one of the children I have worked with over the years, or a picture done by a well-known artist. Suddenly the stillness ends. A jarring schoolwide bell rings and rings, followed by announcements that are piped into every room. The children, for the first time ever, do not welcome the bell, with its promise of freedom: lunch and play. They also frown at the words being spoken to them. Most remarkable of all, the silence returns to the classroom. I am trying hard to think of what to say, but to no avail. I don't want to come back to what we'd been discussing, and I don't know what to mention in connection with the next lesson because, frankly, I haven't figured out what it will be. Finally, the girl who has had us so respectfully attentive speaks: "We should go get our lunch. I'll bet that woman in the picture—I'll bet she got hungry a lot, just like we do!" What a tactful and sensitive way, I think, to link us to the picture, and also to the concreteness of our lives! In no time we were all on our way.

Often when I am sitting with children who are drawing or painting, I realize how much thought they have given to what they want to represent, and even, to why they desire to do so. Sick children have told me, have told their parents, that they want to draw pictures for them so that, in case of the worst, something that matters, that really matters (and was, indeed, hand-made), will be left behind. Only a few months before I wrote these words, a girl dying of bone cancer told her parents that they "could always remember her" by her self-portraits, a dozen or so of which she'd given them over a period of a month. Those pictures showed her steadily thinner and more vulnerable, though always smiling, and always with a sun that also smiled, as if the girl was determined not to yield to an explicit melancholy. This same child, a nurse told me, had drawn pictures of her mother and father, had put tears on both of their faces, tears running down their cheeks. But she had had some second thoughts, had decided to tear up the drawings, had told the nurse that she didn't want to see her parents crying—nor did she want them to see that she had pictured them so mournful.

There is, naturally, a pleasantly casual, spontaneous, quite relaxed and hopeful side to the artwork that many children do—and, of course, some teachers or parents encourage children to be quite conventionally sentimental in their pictorial presentations. "My mother tells me to have the sun smiling, and the flowers big and the grass green as can be, and nice and thick," a boy told my wife, Jane, and me one day. But on occasion he would object: "Usually, I do what she likes—and [what] the teacher [likes], too. But every once in a while, something comes over me, and I just 'let it rip,'" an expression he'd picked up from his airline pilot dad. One of this boy's drawings shows an outburst of a dark sky, with lightning traversing it and thunderclaps (he told us) populating it and trees bent and shivering, it seems, in the rain, and flowers flattened, perhaps by a gust of wind, and a shapeless suggestion of a human form, never completed, observing this decidedly downcast and even ominous landscape. This nine-year-old boy was quick, afterward, to talk a bit about what he had done—and to destroy the evidence, I came to realize, that he mostly didn't want to have around, lest he be prodded by it to start talking in the manner he once did, briefly, while he was finishing a drawing in his classroom: "Sometimes, when there's been a big argument [at home], I look outside and wish it would rain so hard, and thunder so loud that I couldn't hear what they're [his mother and father] saying, and they'd stop, too, because my mom is afraid of lightning and she goes and hides, and my dad would worry about something getting hurt, so he'd check outside, maybe."

"Children's pictures," Anna Freud once said, "are like dreams." She went on to remind her listeners that dreams themselves are pictures, visual scenes, often, to which we attach words. Some patients dream in color and report, not remarks, not warnings or suggestions, or sustained conversation, but rather, what might be called a remembered still life, or a silent motion picture, without a text supplied at the bottom of the frames. She told me of one such patient of hers who favored landscapes, some quite verdant and pleasing to the eye and peaceful, others forbidding, foreboding, dark, so unnerving that the dreamer was woken by a nightmare, a particular landscape. Indeed, to sit with a child, with a classroom full of children, and watch them draw or paint, listen to them as they talk to one another (sometimes, to themselves!) about what they are doing, or trying to do, does not, by any means, assure a spell of sweetness and light. To the contrary, there is a seriousness and an anxiety that commonly accompanies children at work as artists: what to draw, and how to do it well? Additionally, some children, with good reason, worry that they will (to modify the expression) draw too much—let slip some aspect of their life, their thoughts, that ought best be kept out of everyone's sight, their own included.

A boy whose parents were in an extended and truculent struggle over the terms of a divorce drew a picture of his house, as many children in his class were doing. When he had finished, he picked up a red crayon, worked with it rather intently, and announced to his friend sitting across the aisle that he had set fire to the house he'd just drawn. Soon afterward, he picked up a black crayon, crossed out the entire picture, then tore it up. He walked to the teacher's desk and threw the scraps in the nearby wastepaper basket. When he returned, he started on another house, constructed it with painstaking attention to the smallest of details (the keyhole to the front door, a water drainage pipe that ran down the side of the house from the roof and its gutter), and then abruptly stopped working on the drawing. He tore up what he had done, marched with the remnants to the same basket, and threw them in. When he returned to his desk, he announced that he had no more drawings in mind for that day: "I'm getting tired and I have a test later in arithmetic, and I'd rather study for that than do this. And besides, I don't like what I see when I'm finished."

In a sense, that child was speaking for all children when he indicated that to draw, to paint, is to see in several senses: to look at paper; to look at paper as it is filled with one's artistic work; but also to look inward, and thereby, to be given pause—to look hard and long at oneself, one's world, one's worries, and one's prospects. "First I try to picture what I'll draw," a seven-year-old girl often told me. "Then I draw my picture." But there was more to say: "After I'm finished, I look at what

I've done, and sometimes I'm glad, and sometimes I'm not so glad, and sometimes I think I should start over, and sometimes I just don't know, and I want to keep looking until I do know [what to think]. Then my friends look, or the teacher looks, and they show me things I didn't even notice! Then, later, I'll think about what we did in class, and I'll remember the picture—or I might imagine something, and it could be a good picture to do and turn out great, I'll think, if I could do a good job."

In her own unself-conscious manner, this girl was talking about so very much that takes place as children draw and paint. To understand her is to understand concretely the many sides of the child as artist: to contemplate and imagine; to engage one's mind visually; to apply one's skills to a task—an effort rendered, made real by the hands doing their job with as much competence as an individual can muster; to look again—to evaluate and reflect upon one's hopes, one's abilities, as they have been realized; to share a view of the world—a look outward, with others; to let their response become part of one's own awareness, one's sense of things, one's notion of success, or failure; to look inward, yet again, now with one more set of visual experiences to one's credit; to look both backward and forward—hence, to affirm one's rock-bottom humanity. We are the creatures who pause to look, who remember to look, who glance over the shoulder, who foresee, who gaze and peer and stare and wink and blink, and develop various views, who have an overall viewpoint, who behold this life in various ways—our visionary life as it begins with a child's wandering, wondering eyes, unfolds in a child's dreaming life, talking life, picture-making life, and persists until the eyes close for the last time.

Marjorie, a nine-year-old West Virginian, the daughter of a lawyer and grand-daughter of a mine owner, drew a self-portrait meant to evoke her life as a young ballerina. "I love feeling my body do things that it couldn't do before I took ballet lessons! I love the freedom of leaping and jumping and whirling around and around! I forget everything but the steps I'm going to take. It's like flying—that's what I think. In school they told us about gravity—and when I dance, I think: gravity, here I come! I wish I could draw gravity—it would be in a corner, saying, 'I give up,' or it would be running away, with me chasing it! Gravity loses!"

At another moment, upon remembering her return home from ballet lessons, Marjorie likened herself to a Promethean aviator: "I think of someone who has a plane and can fly—that's how I feel sometimes: I'm leaping and flying across the stage. My [ballet] teacher told me to imagine myself holding 'the whole world in my hands,' when I raise my arms, and so I do! 'I've got the whole world in my hands'— that's what I'm thinking there with my arms raised. And my legs are strong, and they're *planted,* so I won't fall, I won't!" Nor has she ever, she announces with pride, as she puts the finishing touches on her drawing of her lithe, exuberant body.

At twelve, Leola had seen very little of the world, even of her own rural Georgia world. A black girl born to poor farming people, she was also paraplegic—and yet: "I can think and I can dream and I can pray and I can let my mind go anyplace it wants, so I've been all over. Mostly, though, I try to stay here and hope God will smile on me, so I can keep my spirits up and show Him it was worth His while, to put me here. Every once in a while, I get in a mood, and I want to go traveling. So I do—I just close my eyes, and I imagine myself with wings, and I'm up there in the sky, like a hawk, and I'm circling and circling, and finally, the good Lord, He will tell me, 'Child, rest your wings (and your legs, too!) and go back home.' So, I do.

"When I pray to God, I'm usually tired at first, because I have to get myself over to the bed [where she likes to pray, and does so four or five times a day] from the chair [where she otherwise sits], and I'm worn down [she crawls, using the considerable power she has developed in her arms], but it doesn't take long for praying to refresh me. I close my eyes, and I'm lost to myself and I'm with God. That's what Nanna [her grandmother] says should happen: 'You leave yourself, Leola, and take that long trip [in prayer] to the good Lord.' When I come back [at the end of her prayer] I feel as if I've been everywhere and I've seen everything—because that's what God is. He's everywhere, and He's everything."

The self-effacement she describes gets worked into her drawing to the point that, as she hands it to me, she lets me know this: "When I'm praying, I'm not me, I'm one of God's little ones." This lesson, learned from devout parents and grandparents, becomes an artist's challenge to realize—a challenge she rose mightily to accept.

Susan is a nine-year-old New Englander, the daughter of an executive who helps run an electronics firm. Both her parents are heavy drinkers, and the family has moved many times in the course of the father's rise to affluence. Susan has had repeated nightmares, and this painting is meant to illustrate one of them: a tornado (in the form of a black sky) has struck, and the girl has hidden underground, but she can't get out because of a green fence that blocks her way. She is shown, small and fragile, both hiding and trying, in vain, to emerge.

Susan asked, rhetorically, as she looked at her effort with paints: "Don't you think people sometimes get caught someplace, and they can't get out?" Immediately, she answered herself: "Maybe someone would come, if that really happened." A pause, then another speculation: "What happened to my parents? Where are they?" She shrugs. She has no answer—though I notice her picking up the paintbrush and washing it free of the black paint she had used last, to represent the tornado-possessed sky.

Betty, who prefers to be called Betsy, a five-year-old Eskimo girl, has pictured a world of fast-flying birds—who, if they cared to notice, would see a snowmobile below them. For Betsy the snowmobile is a powerful, yet tragic object—capable of its own speed and noise, yet hopelessly tied to the confines of the Alaskan tundra. She attributed all sorts of emotions to the machine—a yearning, a pitiful inadequacy, no matter how hard it strives to move upward: "Sometimes, when the [snow]mobile keeps crying and crying [making its noises], I think it's very sad, because it can't fly, like those birds. 'I'd like to join them, but I can't,' it is saying!" She reflects upon the infinity of the divide between a flock in the air, making its way, and a machine, ever earthbound—does so with her fingers, which move across the inch or two between the sky's moving creatures and the land's machine. A worry: "Should I do this [picture] again?" The observer wonders why. The artist replies sensibly: "Well, the distance [between the lowest flying birds and the snowmobile] is not as big as it should be." Later, a reconsideration: "People will know what I'm trying to show." The more I listen to her, the more I hear her mind's poetic attribution, as she tells again and again of a machine's hopes—of soaring skyward, flying and flying. Meanwhile, the birds, with apparently effortless aplomb, make their way elsewhere: "They cover the sky, then they leave for another sky." The tundra, of course, is its own kind of sky, and the birds land there from time to time.

Twelve years old, a hardy Eskimo soul, John took on, by his own description, "a real tough one" when he decided to try to draw, to convey, a tundra wind, hurrying by, in search of an unknowable destination. He tried to do so several times with crayons, felt unpleased with the results. He turned to paints, held the brush a long time, a minute or so, before he wet it with water—then, another minute before he dipped it into the white paint and, later, the black paint. This painting of white and black would be hard to manage even mechanically, as John needed to clean the brush as it moved back and forth from an instrument of lightness to one of darkness. In the end, I realize what an extraordinary achievement John has to his credit. He has struggled for the essence of a subject matter, sent those ominously gray tundra clouds, harbingers of a fierce, howling wind, bearers, often, of snow, as well, racing across the land. He gives us a painting in the abstract expressionist tradition, thinks the heady stranger from another planet: thick white upon thin white, streaks of black, lines white and black.

This artist loves to close his eyes, listen, without other sensory distraction, to a wind that for him talks, boasts, complains, accuses, and in a biblical fashion, exacts its vengeance, all of which he sums up once, with this thought: "Our [Arctic] wind has a mind of its own, my dad says, and you can't really figure it out." Rather, one bows to it, gives it the mighty power that a painting can suggest.

Rose is a nine-year-old Pueblo girl whose affectionate vivacity (I think) prompted her English-born and -reared volunteer teacher at a New Mexico elementary school to designate her as the sole recipient of the phrase "a fine lass." The girl has an evident and passionate attachment to and connection with the land. I watch her, one day, outside, the sun's brilliant light shining upon her and her crayons (we are sitting at a table in a playground), the air so dry one can feel its electric thirst. "I worry about this weather," she tells me. "Even for here, the rain has deserted us." I am taken with her language—the rain's figurative life, its will, and her choice of verbs, a shrewd evocation of the consequences of an action! But she has no interest in spoken performances. She quickly moves from a soulful stare at the land to a rendering of it. She starts her view of the ground from well below its surface, a rabbit's burrow. Rose colors the sandy earth light brown. She works with great care as she constructs plants and bushes, their black roots, their green above-ground life. When she is done she doesn't put the drawing aside or hand it to me; she caresses it: her right palm moves back and forth over the paper, and her face shows a faint smile. Finally she is done, and says: "I like to sit and look at the mesa, and think of all the feet that have visited it. The land must look at us as the ones with two feet covered by shoes!" I suddenly realize what she has told me, that our lower extremities are "seen" as no less than our faces by that Pueblo land, which Rose has just welcomed as a fellow creature, a companion worth all possible respect. "The ground is where the sun's light falls," this girl told me once, and she added: "The ground says thank you, by showing the sun plants and bushes, and once a year, some flowers!"

Later that same day Rose moves her attention upward, begins with a cloud, rather than the sky and the sun (most Anglo children would do the latter), and uses a pencil, first, so she can get just the right, idiosyncratic shape, and if necessary, use an eraser as she strives for a kind of perfection. When satisfied, she calls upon a black crayon. Next, the sky, which she works on carefully, very carefully, wears down the blue crayon noticeably. Rose has left an obvious void—and with a pencil, again, she outlines the sun's circumference, then resorts to the yellow crayon, and finally, for the rays, an orange crayon. A painstaking effort, indeed, I begin to realize, and an effort that reflects a child's enormous respect for the world around her. In case I'd forgotten, she tells me (as she hands over her drawing) what I'd heard from her and other Pueblo children many times: "The sun is the mother of the earth, you know." I return her smile with one of my own, and say, "Yes, I remember." Thus endeth the lesson, I think to myself, about heaven and earth, mother and child.

69

A nine-year-old white New Orleans girl who lives in a lovely, old Garden District home paints a field of flowers and trees, then sequesters some onlookers behind a wall. The year is 1964, and the South is aflame in racial unrest. The girl is attending a private school, is having academic trouble, and decides in her painting to include "some busybodies." She is asked who they might be (by a Yankee doctor who, with the asking, notes in himself a tremor of apprehension, if not self-awareness). The young lady, already proper and refined, replies with initial evasiveness, but without too much delay, gets down to specifics: "Lots of tourists come here [to the neighborhood where she lives and goes to school], and they're always poking around, so we try to keep them away. Thank God we have a wall around our house! Some of them are trying to tell us what's right, and they point their fingers at us, as though they know everything and we don't know anything! They're all wrong, but they think they're right! If they'd just mind their own business, it would be better—the 'agitators'!"

She is asked pointedly why she paints the "tourists" or "agitators" black. She replies quietly, tersely: "I don't know." She is asked if she is referring, thereby, to "Negroes," the word then in use for such discussions. "No," she answers, right away —and then this elaboration: "It's all of 'them,' the people who keep telling you that they want to change everything, and you should do something different." She had just been told as much by her own teacher, so she had announced earlier in a matter-of-fact manner. This remonstrance of nameless others, in contrast, is a heated one, indeed.

In Texas, ten-year-old Carmen, the daughter of humble Spanish-speaking farm workers, records the pain of being asked by an Anglo schoolteacher why she doesn't ever seem to change her dress: "She told me I'm always wearing it, the same one." There is no other dress for her, and she takes good care of what she has, washing it every other day. Carmen's picture gives the viewer that teacher in her own many-flowered dress. Beside the teacher is a nameless woman harvester, whom the girl begins to offer a green dress, only to have second thoughts, so she does not follow through on the initiative. The teacher has large, peering, penetrating eyes ("She stares at us a lot"), a big toothy mouth, and at her side is a black bird, a vulture, Carmen lets me know. The agricultural worker is noticeably shorter, seems suspended in air—the ground and even her feet are cut out from under her! This is someone whose mouth is as thin as possible (it has to be firmly kept shut) and who lacks ears: "I wish I didn't even hear some of the things that teacher says to us," Carmen exclaimed one day. But the sun seems kindly—for, as the girl once said: "They [the Anglos] may own the land, but not the sky, and not the sun, and not the moon, and not the stars." The enumeration was precisely, happily made—a child's determined, heartfelt search for some kind of equity in this world.

A thirteen-year-old Eskimo youth, Miriam, has dreamed that she flew to Washington, D.C., and there saw the Lincoln Memorial, a building celebrated by both her teacher and her minister. She had been shown a picture of it at school, and had heard a long lecture on Lincoln's virtues. In the dream, she saw many steps, all of them white marble, and then the statue of the sitting president, who spoke some words to her, which she forgot, promptly, upon waking. Indeed, the president began to disappear, too, as she got out of bed and tried to hold on to what had crossed her mind in the dark: "I forgot the dream completely by the time I was on my way to school, but as soon as I came near [the building], I remembered that [in the dream] I'd just flown to our nation's capital and met the best president we ever had! The trouble was, he got killed, just when America needed him most, after the Civil War ended!

"When people die, they go someplace—way away. They may visit us—in a dream, like I had. My daddy says: 'When you dream, that means you're having visitors.' Maybe Lincoln would like us here [in the Eskimo community] to be better people!"

When she has finished her painting, I ask her about Lincoln: Where is he in it? She is not in the least taken aback by the president's apparent absence, or my surprise that such is the case. "You don't need a statue to remember someone. You can do it yourself!" Upon hearing those words, I let my eyes dwell on the arctic white she mobilized in honor of a fallen moral hero of long ago, who has visited her in the darkness of night and whom she has brought to this moment of personal, introspective light.

In Kasserine, one of Tunisia's towns, a twelve-year-old boy, Habib, lets his imagination have full reign as he constructs an ideal community, a world of harmony: "Everyone will be kind to everyone else, and everything will work, and no one is in trouble." He is in a classroom taught by a friend of my son Bob's, who has been talking with children about their Islamic faith. Habib gives Bob a lecture about faith, its importance in each person's life. He asks Bob whether he, a medical student, prays regularly. Bob candidly says no, at least not in a conventional, explicit way—that is, not in a church building. Habib makes a point of constructing a mosque, colors it green, the color of Islam's paradise, and tells Bob that all the other people shown, busy with their everyday lives, take time to go and pray. The boy's passionate commitment to detail, his large patience with himself and the demands of his vision, is rewarded, finally, by the breadth, the scope of this extraordinary scene, so intricately and compellingly presented. The boy has taken hours to do his work, has several times closed his eyes, as if to conjure up a particular aspect of the human landscape he intends to represent for himself, for his American visitor. "It is my duty to tell you all I can— to show it to you the best way I can," he lets Bob know. The *duty* of meticulous visual representation, documentation—a pictorial assertion of a child's energetically utopian introspection!

At ten, Gordon enjoyed a comfortable life. His parents were quite well off and well educated. They lived in a prosperous neighborhood, and the boy attended a fine private school. But others, white and black alike, lived another kind of life, he certainly knew—and he worried about the fate of these age-mates and fellow citizens, utter strangers. He knew that a nearby northern city was then experiencing a good deal of racial turmoil, a consequence of an ambitious effort at school desegregation—the busing of black students to hitherto all-white schools. The bused children were not greeted with any great enthusiasm. Before Gordon drew this picture he asked a rhetorical question that has resounded throughout history: "Why do people act so mean to other people?" I didn't have to try to answer. He had a thought or two: "I guess it's because they're unhappy. When that happens, you look for trouble, and you find it—someone to kick or hit when you feel down." With that said, he pursued visually his sense of what was happening—fearful black children being brought daily by bus to schools inhabited by angry, distrustful white children, some of them ready to fight on behalf of what they considered to be their turf. Gordon finished the yellow bus first, then added some brown to it, even as, with the same crayon, he pictured two quite fragile, vulnerable black children peering out of windows. The front of the bus seems to suggest a requirement of force, as in a snub-nosed pistol, or a battering ram. (In fact, the police were everywhere, struggling to keep peace in the midst of mounting violence.) As for the whites, they are big, even hefty, and one has a quite evident club. They are in front of the old schoolhouse, defenders of their faith. "It's a war," Gordon tells me, with a sigh, as he hands me the drawing. He is "sure," he adds, that were he in the shoes of the black students, he'd "play hooky." Gordon knows the white students are scared, too (he has heard such psychological comment at home from his parents), but he can't help wondering "even so, why they have to fight." In a remarkable reflection, he wonders whether, under some set of circumstances, he, too, might be made anxious or fearful enough to want to pick up a stick and use it as a club against someone.

At ten, Morton already had learned to take Judaism quite seriously. He had not only attended Hebrew school faithfully; he had contemplated certain important moments in his people's history, and especially that time of encounter between God and Moses. There he is, Moses atop the mountain, his arm outstretched, touching the tablets, with their commandments, their message of instruction as to how to live this life. He stands on the ledge of sorts, mentioned in the Bible, while a flight of birds in a collective arrow points toward him. Below, his fellow Jews are standing aside the golden calf, a symbol of their idolatrous ways, the star of David as a torso for each person—an artist's wonderfully idiosyncratic statement. For Jews, God is beyond artistic representation or characterization, yet a child's mind contends with its own imperatives: to see as well as say, to picture as well as declare. Morton's resolution of a kind—a segment of a limb, which he calls "God's paw." With extraordinary concentration Morton describes the exchange, the red strands emanating from the paw becoming the red text of the Decalogue: lines of communication. The red on the head of Moses tells us that he is surely in tune, mind and soul, with what his hand is holding. Meanwhile, the sun's yellow, the light of the world, radiates from the "paw," illuminates the text, suffuses the two parties to this charged moment of moral communion. The boy adds a contemporary thought to his picture, reminding a twentieth-century psychiatrist how troubled the Lord was at the spectacle of thoughtlessness and self-preoccupation below, only to be reassured by Moses with a gesture of "support" (to use a word so much favored today—almost as though psychotherapy was at work "up there," as well as divine intervention). But soon we are back to the drawing, marveling at the way Morton uses a dark blue to encase the commandments, as if they came out of the sky, the firmament. This boy has made an utterly distant and elusive past thoroughly concrete and endowed it with a rich and subtle grace.

moses →

Clouds fascinate many children, regardless of their background. Indian children are especially responsive to clouds and watch them closely, endowing them with special qualities. "Clouds are spirits traveling—our ancestors," Gerry, a thirteen-year-old Pueblo lad, points out, even as he points with his right forefinger toward the sky, filled that afternoon with more than a few low-flying cumulus clouds. He takes on the challenge of representing those clouds on paper, not so easy to do for many children. He hesitates for a while, speaks of aesthetic problems—how to put white on white, for instance. Then he frees himself of such a constraint, lets his imagination take over. He works with blue and black and gray, blends and shades his colors, and finally, seems through. At that moment he is holding a black crayon in his right hand, up and away from the paper, poised to let go, I think, because his left hand is moving the paper slightly away. But then both hands stay with the job: the left moves the paper back, closer, and the right moves the crayon back toward the center of the clouds. As if an emissary of those hands, the voice announces: "I'm not through yet." He plants a black dot, looks at it, expands upon it, presses hard, whereupon the crayon breaks. He is chagrined. I reassure him, tell him many, many crayons have broken in all the years of such work—and, in fact, far fewer since I've been in New Mexico, talking with young people like him, who tend to be gentle, indeed, when drawing. He relaxes, uses the smaller rather than larger piece of black crayon (a becoming modesty, thoughtfulness) and develops his black dot further. When he is through, he sees perplexity on my face and explains: "A plane." Often, he has looked up, both marveling at planes above yet wondering where they're all going, and why so many fly so constantly. His wry comment, once: "The Anglos are always in a big hurry." This time he says: "I hope the plane doesn't hurt the clouds; I hope they get out of its way." I am left with an image of clouds energetically scurrying to make a path for yet another modern projectile.

A twelve-year-old Eskimo boy, John, shows the thrust of ice, its massive presence and power, and is convinced that nowhere else does such imposing height present itself. He eventually learns otherwise from his teachers but discards their factuality with a firm vote of confidence in his own life's experiences: "They have read books— but they haven't seen the ice I have seen." He is right, too. They most certainly have read books, and they have not traveled, as he has, to places along the Arctic coastline which offer dramatic monuments to the stubborn congealed coldness that he celebrates.

Those ice floes stir the boy, turn his mind to a calm reverence, to a kind of awe, to inwardness: an examination of nature's constantly changing sameness. "When you see the ice [floes], you should remember that they grow, or they get smaller and smaller, but they don't go away. They don't remain the same, but they remain! I've wondered if I could climb them, but that is not for us—the birds, the [polar] bears, not us. I've imagined myself walking on them, and waving back at people—and they're standing [on the shore] waving at me."

He is pleased with his mastery of technique, putting white on the white paper, and he loves displaying the arctic blue of the water that miraculously, he cares to observe, "holds up all that ice." He wonders at the water's strength: "The ice is strong, but the water is the winner!" A contest is taking place in his watercolor. Were people and one of their boats to intrude on this scene, he announces, they'd be represented by a small circle, almost invisible amid the enormity of the floes. But he decides to keep human beings out of this far northern seascape.

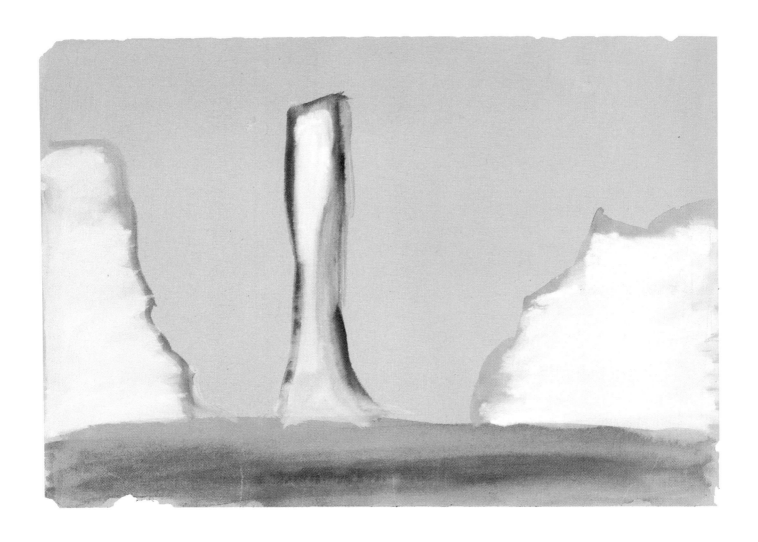

When John, a Hopi boy, was eleven, he wondered why, at certain moments, the Arizona sky was so clear and sunny, so reassuring in its blanket of warmth, whereas in a flash (and sometimes *with* a flash) it seemed that darkness would descend on the sacred tribal land. The noise from above frightened him, even as it excited him, and the bolts of lightning, especially, gave him much to contemplate: "My grandfather told me that the lightning is someone's weapon, stolen from the sun. A spirit has snatched a tiny part of the sun, and run away with it, and then he throws it across the sky before he gets burned up by it." Quite a story, I think, and a hard one to tell visually, so the boy decides, as he sets out to evoke a drama taking place high above: dark clouds, thunderheads, on their way to a collision, with the sun, suddenly small and weak, caught helplessly in between—yet, with its patch of surrounding blue sky, also a promise of what will come, soon enough, because, as John reminds a New Englander, "The storms come fast, but they go fast. They tire out and give up."

The boy wants to register the fierce howl of the wind, does so by bearing down with his black crayon, making circular lines, or vinelike lines, creating a box of sorts, filled with lines of parallel shading, an enclosure of vehemence, of energy demanding exit. "Don't worry," he tells me (and, I decide, he is assuring himself, too, for he is nervously scratching his right arm with his left fingers and his left leg is twitching a bit), "no one will get hurt." I don't question his statement, but still he indicates that I need some educational assistance: "We know how to protect ourselves in storms— they sweep across our land, but they don't take us with them. We wait for the sun, and it always comes back to us." He lets that explanation rule the day, rule his drawing. He titles it "The Waiting Sun."

In Atlanta, early in the 1980s, a time when America was at peace yet many worried about a nuclear war between the Soviet Union and the West, a twelve-year-old girl, Sue, the daughter of white, upper-middle-class parents much involved in what was then called "the antiwar movement," sits down with paints to evoke what she most anxiously dreads, what she fears as if it were an imminent possibility, if not a likelihood: the consequences of a nuclear explosion in the midst of her native Atlanta. "It would be *terrible*," she says, and then, unsatisfied with the adequacy of the word, she repeats it three times, meanwhile working away with her paintbrush, with the paints, with the bowl of water and piece of cloth nearby, which enable her to be rid of one color, turn to another. She starts with black—the overall darkness of the moment, the horror. Then she moves to yellow—the sun's rays, soon to be overcome by a virtually everlasting tragedy. Next, she calls upon red and orange, pursues a grisly portrayal of limbs and torsos scattered, of blood everywhere: in sum, enormous destruction of life, of property, to the point of chaos—of a kind she takes pains, however, to evoke, to render for herself, for me, to see, to discuss, to ponder. She asks: "Do you realize how awful it would be?" I reply: "Yes, but I have to admit, I find it hard to do so." She nods. She understands my "problem"! That is why she did what she did, made that painting, its surreal nature a reminder (to me, to others) of what might (at any moment, she believes) become all too real.

My son Bob and I are sitting with a girl in a Tennessee church's Sunday school, and she is talking about Jesus—His great love "for people who weren't popular." The girl is in the sixth grade, but young for such an academic level, "only nine and a half," she tells us with some pride. She is known to be exceptionally bright. She is also, we learn, spiritually introspective. She tries to imagine what it was like in the Holy Land, so many centuries ago, when the man Jesus, a carpenter, walked the land with his friends: fishermen, peasants, ordinary folk, some hurt and ailing, some even hungry, and some, she reminds us, exceedingly unpopular, even unloved, even very much disliked. Her child's heart goes out to "those kinds of people," she tells us, and it is the teachings of Jesus that prompt such a response. She decides not to draw the conventional pictures of Jesus, or of well-known biblical scenes, moments. She closes her eyes for three or four seconds, then begins, working so swiftly, with such confidence, that we wonder whether she hasn't planned the portrait that emerges well in advance. Who is "Dorie"? No one in particular, we are told. But in case there be any doubt, her essential attribute is noted beside the drawing. Whose heart is under that fairly hot sun? It is Dorie's—but why is it green, not red? The artist, Gretchen, doesn't know, precisely—but then again, maybe she does know: "Well, she's still young." A green-hearted girl, not yet full of the heart's red passion, is already a purple woman, that is, sinful, her eyes sending messages of calculation and shyness; earlier suffering becomes contemporary isolation. Her arms, behind her back, make a circle. Will she ever escape that encirclement, or is her destiny sealed? The artist silently wonders, and wants us also to do so. Then Gretchen declares: "I hope she gets out of the trouble she is in, but I don't know if she will." After such spoken empathy, emphatic silence. We continue to want more, though, pressing for details, for a story. Gretchen demurs, won't comment upon her choice of colors, her "thoughts" (as we phrased it) with regard to what she has so dramatically pictured. My son Bob, a tactful gentleman, lets the matter drop. He is grateful for a child's wonderfully suggestive effort. I am, alas, frustrated—hence a mannerism of the clinic: I ask about the *artist,* wonder whether she has friends, is happy at school. "I'm fairly popular," Gretchen declares, justifiably surprised at this turn in the conversation. I go no further, but afterward I linger silently on her adverbial qualification, and its role in this affecting, provocative visual statement.

Dorie
the
girl
nobody
loved

In Crystal City, Texas, in "the valley," the area north of the Rio Grande, a ten-year-old Anglo boy, Peter, extols his dad's business sense, his industriousness, his essential decency and kindness toward others, his many generous contributions to charities. But his father has also been engaged in a struggle: "Union people," as the boy describes them, have tried to "organize the plant," a factory where raincoats and rainhats are made. The boy is fiercely loyal to his father, sees him as an embattled hero, eager to be productive and successful, but thwarted by those who "want more than they deserve," a phrase the parent has handed down to the child as an explanation of why some workers are engaged in a determined strike.

"I guess this is what is happening," Peter tells me after he has taken a pencil and sketched his dad's factory and a combative scene outside. Gun-wielding strikers are ready to assault the guards his father has hired, who are shown with shields. (In fact, the real Spanish-speaking strikers walked not with guns but with picket signs in their hands.) The boy is about to declare his drawing done but suddenly has an important afterthought. He sketches an American flag, connected to a pole, which he proudly perches on the factory roof. Then he says: "My dad loves this country, and he's ready to go and fight for it. He was in the army, and he says that was the best time of his life—and he learned to fight, and he will if those guys [the strikers] make him." Peter smiles for the first time as he tells me, in addition, of his own willingness to "stand tall" for his dad. That phrase comes easily, naturally, to him.

In Managua, Nicaragua, Marie, who is eleven, talks of Good Friday, "the most important day in the whole year." She has drawn many pictures of "Him," but she wants to do another—Him on His way to His death. She constructs a story for herself—Jesus is told that He will soon enough be hanging from a newly made cross, which He will have to carry. "I don't know exactly how it happened, but it happened in Jerusalem," she says. She thinks that maybe He walked a "long time," and then "got to a hill," and that was where "He was crucified, and it took three hours before He died." She struggles to create a path for Jesus—decides to color it blue, notes to herself aloud that her road resembles a river. She makes a connection between the ancient Roman Empire and Nicaragua today: "There were fights then, and we have fights. The leader ordered Jesus to die, and our leaders do that to people. If you cause trouble, you can be put in prison, and then they'll kill you."

Jesus and His crown of thorns, and His cross, and His fate that day are the subject of a child's drawing and also a matter she connects to her own life, never mind that of her country under the Sandinistas: "We're poor, but my father and mother really believe in Jesus, more than the government. They say they're ready to die fighting [on behalf of their religious beliefs], if they have to stay away from church to please the [government] officials. I think Jesus must be crying for all of us here, who love Him, but we have to wipe away His tears!" I wonder aloud how that is done. The brief answer: "If we believe in Him, then He won't be sad about us." So it goes, a child's faith, her spiritual introspection, connected to pictorial representation.

For James, twelve, and his family, quite well-to-do people who lived in a fine New Orleans neighborhood, the angry people who besieged two elementary schools in another section of the old, cosmopolitan port city in the fall of 1960 were a people apart, a "mob." The boy's parents were "embarrassed," they kept on saying, by the national attention such street behavior brought to their city. Working-class white people responded angrily, sometimes violently, to a federal judge's order that school desegregation must, at last, start. The issue before the city—before the entire nation— was, of course, one of race, yet the issue was also one of class, something this boy well knew, and conveyed in his roundup, of sorts, a lasso meant to encircle a motley crew, whom he described this way: "They're the 'riffraff' [a term his parents used], and a lot of them, they're probably drinking, even in the morning—alcoholics. They're pulling our city down—our reputation. My dad says it's a real tragedy, and it could hurt business."

His parents had taken him to watch the scene—observe and hear hundreds of men, women, children, shout obscenities at a lone black child, Ruby Bridges, as she entered the Frantz School. James kept talking, thereafter, about a city being "pulled down"—and now he reacts, goes on the offensive, does some pulling of his own, ropes in the "mob," and says, upon finishing the job, "There!" His next poignant remark: "I guess it's not so easy [to do] in real life."

Only ten, Pam, the daughter of a prominent white Alaskan, is quite sensitive to the life of an Eskimo maid, Mary, who works for her family, and for her, as well, as she points out: "She spends more time with our family than [with] her own. She takes good care of me—and sometimes I feel as though I'm taking her away from *her* children, and that's not nice!" This quite sensitive, idealistic girl dares to put herself in Mary's mind as she tries to picture her. The scene is the child's bedroom, with Mary beside a chair both she and Pam like to use. Nearby is a window, nicely draped with curtains that Mary has always admired—and beyond, the blue of the sea. Mary is made watchful, with eyes that dominate her face. Her hands are folded in front of her; she is looking, as she often does, within: "I wonder a lot what she's thinking. Maybe she's home [in her mind], with her kids, instead of being here with us, having to listen to our silly talk all day." (I notice, a little later, the favor extended Mary: no ears, an immunity from that "silly talk"!)

A drawing of a child's compassionate empathy, done with a schematic minimalism, a critic might say: the musing, observant maid, the chair she favors, the view that carries her toward the family she sees only infrequently—all taking place in a room emphatically not her own, as the owner of the room is frank to acknowledge. In a sense, that owner is making a drawing not just of a maid's yearning, but of her own discomfort.

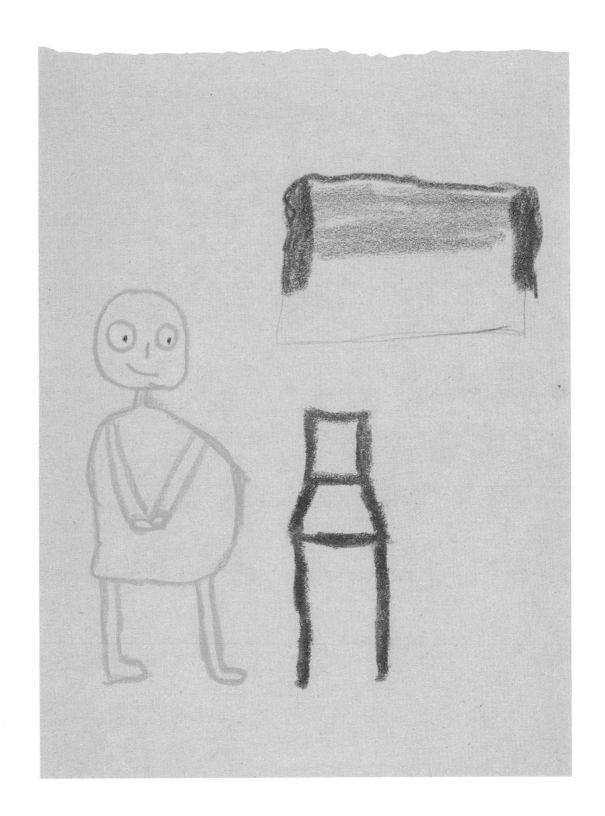

Larry appears at some length in the text, and here he is again, now (at age nine) offering his father, who is surveying his land, acres and acres of it, the row upon row of crops represented by the horizontal and vertical lines: an agricultural empire. The sun is more subdued, less grasping than in the earlier picture, meant to show its power over the land, over those who work it, but it is unmistakably Larry's sun: the points, the fingers on its circumference—his signature. The father has a black hat, not unlike the cowboy one he used to wear, and the black shoes resemble his riding shoes. He is big-shouldered, has reddish blond hair—and here, his back is to the viewer: he surveys the land, and we look at him doing so. "My daddy loves his land," Larry told me once, then he smiled, and frankly acknowledged how unnecessary that remark had been: "I know you know that." Still, he had made that point again, for himself—and he had let me know how important that land was to a man who seems rather diminished by it. Larry's "daddy," as he always called him, was sometimes called "Big Daddy" by the handful of foremen who were friendly enough with him to use that rural Southern expression. He *was* fatherly with those men, who were as loyal to him as that term of endearment implied. The migrant workers were another matter, quite literally—not really people to Larry's daddy, as his son well knew. "If I'd have put those folks [the migrants] in there [the scene he'd drawn], I'd have made Daddy bigger. That's how they see him!" So it goes, the artist's sense of proportion— a response to his sense of political, economic, social, and racial reality.

Nine-year-old Larry of the Florida agribusiness world returns once more—now with his uncomplimentary view of the fancy private school he attended as a child. In fact, the building was tan stucco, but he turns it into red brick, almost windowless. He did not like his teachers there, or the principal. In class he had stood up for the poor of the world, for the migrants his own father employed, and the result was a scornful dismissal from all those educators. The boy senses at work the hard, cold, even crude facts of life: teachers bowing to one of the county's big shots, a wealthy grower with many connections in the sheriff's office, among other places. "The teachers took the side of Daddy, and his friends, and all I was saying was, 'If you listen to what they tell you in church about Jesus, and what He said—then it's better off to be poor.'"

A boy's innocent, literal-minded attentiveness to Scripture turned into a family's crisis, a school's as well. The boy repaired his home life, but views his teachers with a new skepticism: "They tell you what you should think about everything, not just the subjects they teach!" He is regarding the school as a prison, the doors as an entry to a prison, the window with a featureless face and neck or upper torso, as offering a restricted glimpse to that person. The sky is thin, the sun, usually so important to him, nowhere to be found. The enormous building fills the paper, fills the air, perhaps to preclude anyone's independent life. It is a greedily expansive place, for sure, and a place that has no ground underneath, as if we are in the presence of an institution that aims to be everywhere—a cold, forbidding omnipresence.

Snow fascinates Jean, nine; she looks at it with tenderness, with wonder, even with awe, and calls it a gift: "It is sent to us, so we can all stop and be happy that our land has been covered." A moment's hesitation, then a terse comparison: "Their snow plows are already out." She is referring to the New Mexico highway department, its desire to clear snow from the roads. Many times she and others in her Pueblo family have made the comparison between their desire to behold the snow and the urgent wish that "Anglos" have "to push it here and push it there, pile it up, in big piles," and not only on the nearby roads, but up the mountains: "They want to ski, so they get the snow out of the way [on the mountain roads], so they can jump all over it. The poor snowflakes!" I suddenly, for the first time, see her view of skiing—plastic descending with great force on the fragile particularity of those miraculous snowflakes, each with its own dignity and beauty—in what seems to be a purely aesthetic effort, worked at painstakingly, with white crayon on black paper. (I often bring paper of different colors to children, and occasionally, for one reason or another, they don't choose white.) Yet, as I connect her picture to her remarks, I realize the implication of this artistic effort—a major political statement, a cultural comparison.

Jean, nine, has given us snowflakes and now offers an incarnation of the invisible, a spring zephyr, a wind that, as she puts it, "combs the trees . . . brushes the land . . . sweeps through . . . whistles hello . . . then the silence of good-bye." I delete only a few connective phrases, words, distractions that conceal a child's lyrical commentary on her lyrically wrought landscape. Later, she points out to me how challenging the wind that she celebrates can be to those trees: "You know, trees can be lazy, like us. The wind is a reminder to get exercise, not [just] stand there. The wind makes the tree bend. The wind makes the branches go up and go down, up and down. My grandmother says the tree is much stronger after the wind has blown. The tree loses its weak branches. The wind tests the tree, and if the tree can't meet the test, that is the end: the tree falls down."

Prompted by Jean, I think of her three trees as visitors to a gym, getting a strenuous workout, courtesy of a taskmaster, the wind. She extends her imagery, reminds me of how the wind descends upon the land, "cleans things up there." Her verbs, her descriptions, are arresting, and later I am struck by their lyrical, vivid power. She has become the wind, even as her picture captures it—the vast sky, full of an action that is realized in the trees and, yes, in the slightly aroused land, with its delicately jagged rather than flat surface. A quiet, introspective child who belongs to a peaceful people manages to evoke a good deal of energetic perturbation.

With paints, Carmen, at ten, describes a world, dreams of a world. In the Rio Grande Valley she knows the poverty, the marginality of Chicano field hands—yet she dares see herself staking out land, standing against a pole, thereby asserting herself in the tradition of Texas homesteaders: this is mine, and I will stand up for it, fight for it, if necessary. The sky is a deep blue with no sun, and some ominously dark birds, which "may be" vultures, with their quite evident beaks, Carmen acknowledges. On the other hand, she speculates, they could "turn out to be hawks," a favorite of her father's, with that wonderful glide they display.

Land lives constantly in her mind—a desire to own it as well as work it, to build on it, rather than help others, one grower after another, build their fortune: "They [the agribusiness people] have huge places, but I only want a small farm, and I'd do everything on it myself, and I'd never complain!" Her right arm is extended, a gesture emphasizing that cry of hers, that call to opportunity for herself, for the family she dreams of bringing up as stable, hardworking farmers, rather than migrants, at the constant call of others.

A Swedish boy, Martin, at the age of twelve, has a religious sensibility that owes more to Calvin than to Luther. "It's either in heaven or hell that we'll end up," he tells us in fluent, if accented, English, and it's all been decided, I think. When, and by whom? "God" is his answer, of course, and as for the time, "Maybe even before we're born, I don't know." But he knows enough to be able to engage in rather sophisticated theological discussion. Yes, we might have some possible say in the matter, through our deeds, through the manner in which we live our lives. Nonetheless, this lad does wonder whether God, who has "all power" over us, over everything and everyone, doesn't have His own preconceptions, if not definite conclusions as to the outcome for each of us. While I think of Calvin's *Institutes,* Martin draws the fires of hell, the ultimate blackness of that kind of judgment, a fateful condemnation, indeed. As for heaven, "It is hard to know how to picture it!" The boy moves on the same piece of paper, interestingly enough (he might have used another piece, available to him), from the fires of the inferno to a paradise that is almost invisible to the eye: very soft, indistinct, yellow and blue shadings. As if to make a distinction clear, the boy draws a line, with a pencil, aided by a ruler. Then he regrets the act—and in a breathtaking spiritual reversal, worthy perhaps of contemporary bourgeois Sweden, muses: "It's hard to know where hell ends and heaven begins!" He is talking about his picture, needless to say—but, in fact, he doesn't say so. Rather, he tells us that God Himself, sometimes, must have a perplexed moment or two: "I wonder whether He wants to make subdivisions in both places [in heaven and hell], because people are different, very [different]." This Dante of the late twentieth century even thinks about drawing some of those "subdivisions" but surrenders to the overwhelming human complexity of the matter, puts aside decisively the box of crayons and the paper.

Sam belongs to the Pueblo nation, and at thirteen tries hard to remember its messages as well as the Anglo ones he has learned to recognize as so important. Once he tried to envision the essence of the evening sky, not through morphology, but as light, which he wanted in a mystical way to liberate from darkness. To do so, he called upon all the available tools, a mixed media of sorts: crayons and paints both, but most important, a mind ready to establish its own message with colors powerfully suggestive. The clouds glimmer, shine, through white paint as the moon touches them. The stars possess their own haunting blue light. The moon abandons its distinctive borders, merges its yellow with the evening's dark strands of being. All things touch, blend, into light's shadowy self. "I look up there," Sam says in an almost hushed voice, an evening voice, "and I see the night racing ahead of the day, but the day will catch it, and wipe it out—only for a while, though." No victory is complete, and amid darkness and light, both, he would tell me at some length, there is always "the hunt" going on, the chase that we define with temporal words (*night* and *day*), or geographical ones (*moon* and *sun*), and which he tries to approach, rather than define, with hints, intimations enabled by color, by the way it is arranged.

Another time Sam has been staring and staring at several clouds as they make their way across the sky. One of them blocks the sun temporarily, but soon moves on: "I wonder if it [the cloud] got burned," the boy softly asks himself as he prepares to draw yet another sky. He once again dismisses the realist tradition, labors hard to work the sun's yellow into the atmospheric blue, and notes a certain greenish consequence: "I didn't plan on that [happening]." Then he picks up a black crayon, reminds himself of what he has heard, that clouds, too, have "a birth," and so the dots: "They are just starting out, and they'll grow!" He is excited at that prospect, looks upward, as if he might actually see what he has just rendered, then realizes something: "You can't see clouds being born, only see them when they grow up." Visible clouds are adults, I think, as I follow his eyes' lead, lift my head to gaze: the mystery of growth everywhere to contemplate.

A Hopi girl, Miriam, nine years old, has a subtle, nuanced eye for even the smallest shifts in the environment—changes of weather, of vegetation, the ups and downs of the terrain. She remembers certain stones, doesn't "disturb" them as others do, by picking them up, feeling them, throwing them down. She prizes every tree she knows—an individual for whom each hour's progression through the day deserves attentive, affectionate regard. She welcomes the sun's heat, expresses admiration for it, and gratitude, as well. Once she tried to convey that solar energy, its flowering impact on a favorite tree of hers, nestled amid two hills and surrounded by precious grass, each blade of which, for Miriam, deserves to be upheld as a reminder of the world's promises that are, indeed, fulfilled, again and again.

The child draws that grass ever so carefully, and the tree, too. She seems to enjoy shading the hills a reddish brown and lets the valley slope to the bottom of the page at one point. The sun is made of circular loops, which remind me of an electric stove's coil—so hot the blue sky seems to be fading. "Well," says the young artist, as she looks at her own picture, "I guess each leaf on the tree is waving kisses to the sun." It is this kind of thinking that Miriam summons often, but especially when she goes to that particular valley, sits on a favorite rock, thinks about the world—her past ancestors, her contemporary friends and relatives, her future as one of the many "spirits," which, she is sure, hover nearby.

Earlier in these pages Dicky appeared as the eleven-year-old artist who drew a black boy in a ghetto setting—the artist with a great, kindly interest in others less fortunate than himself. In a painting prompted by the prospect of a busing program that would bring poor city children to the quite well-to-do town Dicky has always called his own, we see a boy's shrewd anticipatory fears (and they would prove to be uncannily correct forecasts). Two orange-red boys frolic at soccer in a schoolyard, a gym building nearby, while a black boy, one foot in the woods, one on the grass, stands a good distance away. The trees loom high, the first signs of green spring upon their branches, the boy notes (it is a cold, late April day). The sky is dark, sunless. When Dicky is done, he turns, gazes out the window at a large, well-kept field. He has used his paintbrush rather quickly, almost hurriedly, as if he is impatient. He is troubled by the subject matter, he tells me, and also worries that he hasn't done a good job with the paints he has just used. I don't agree at all. The sight of that black child stays with me a long time—the movement within his body, the active, slightly desperate agility. He is a diminutive fellow aside a natural world yet to turn warm and inviting, a natural world that looms, that threatens to overpower. Meanwhile, the other two boys, so clearly bigger, so assured, so in the middle of things, center stage, have fun as they keep kicking the black ball around.

Joshua is his name, a nine-year-old black child who lives in one of Baltimore's poorer neighborhoods—poor in so many ways, but not poor, for Joshua, so far as religious life goes. His parents have named him after the ancient biblical figure, a man of moral and military leadership, the boy knows. He also knows about the battle of Jericho and the Lord's promise that its walls would collapse if the Jewish army at the gates not only massed its fighting strength, but went through certain rituals over a span of days, including the blowing of horns. "They have their trumpets," Joshua tells us, and my son Bob and I say yes with a certain vague memory of the story. The boy then connects the distant past to his present: "I play the trumpet. When I play, a lot of the time, I think of Jericho, the walls—they 'came tumblin' down,' like we say, we sing, in church!"

He wants to draw those walls, and he does. He uses a ruler at certain points, to ensure the orderly construction of a formidable wall. When he is finished he goes into his bedroom and brings out his trumpet. He blows it for half a minute or so, then puts it down, picks up a red crayon, indicates fires, and with a line, indicates a fissure, as well: the wall has begun to collapse as surely as the one thousands of years ago did. Joshua is a boy who has learned to take ever so seriously a particular religious tradition, and who enacts it with crayons, with a trumpet—his name given a resounding and visible reality!

A Pueblo boy of thirteen, Gerry, lives north of Santa Fe, and works hard with a pencil: "I like it better than all those crayons—too many colors!" He talks as he draws, and delivers a soliloquy after he has finished. "The tree gets lonely sometimes, but usually it's glad to be alone! When it's tired, the branches bend down, but mostly they're waving a little with the wind, or just saying hello to us. Birds stop by, and some live there for a while. The branches say hello, and the birds say hello, and the next thing you know, they're together." When he and I walk, I note that he looks carefully at the real-life tree he had in mind when he drew—he doesn't take it for granted— and even says an audible hello while passing. For a long time I looked for a person to be the recipient of the greeting—only to learn, finally, that I was with a child who constantly addressed nature, in many ways, and only sometimes in its human aspect.

In León, Nicaragua, Pablo (who is twelve years old and two days, he informs us) decides to draw what he most likes, having been asked to do just that: "Oh, whatever you most like." His answer, a delightful echo: "Oh, I will." He gives the paper a house, a tree, some land productively used for crops, the mountains and a sun peering beyond. The boy has worked deliberately, assiduously, stopping several times to close his eyes, summon images, it seems. He has a plan; he executes it. When he is finished he hands his drawing over. I note its distinctive character—the beauty of those mountains, the wonderful integration of the sun with them, but also a failure to connect what is below, the house and trees and land. He explains that he is putting down what he most likes, in accordance with the request made! But, in fact, he has his own, original arrangement, manner of presentation, and I have been presumptuous, interfering, condescending in my inability, my refusal, to let him have his particular say, with my all too conventional wish to see some land, perhaps, connecting the house, the trees, the garden. I'm a little curious about his mountaintops, so nicely wrought. I put my finger on them, whereupon he smiles, and says if God wanted to "come back," he could do so on one of them; they're landing pads of sorts. I note the left window of the house, outlined in black, and then remember that his mother has an injured right eye, and then realize that it is the house's *right* window I have been contemplating.

Marjorie's father, a prominent and public-spirited West Virginia lawyer, is pictured standing on top of a Charleston bank building. The girl was only seven when she made the painting, but she knew to imply, more than imply, her father's wealth, his social distinction, too: he stands tall, indeed, his head touching the sky, his face tilted upward, the sun his neighbor. "My daddy has lots of things to do," the second-grader tells me as she sits in a classroom. "He likes to go climbing, and then he thinks, and makes his decisions," she adds. Marjorie (the ballerina who appears in an earlier picture) has her own wide views to take in from a home high on a particularly attractive hill. In a distinct nod to her Appalachian origins, she wonders about those who lack such an advantage: "If you live someplace that's flat, you can't see much, and that's no good." Her father has told her as much. He needs, every once in a while, to look out of the windows of the building that he calls his (and partially owns) in order to "stop and think." Marjorie explains: "Daddy doesn't like to buy things [stocks] unless he knows 'the big picture.'" That last phrase she has heard used by her parents as they converse—and, in a sense, her picture presents a picture of a parent searching for a "picture."

An important white banker in Clarksdale, Mississippi, employs in his home a maid, Sally. His daughter, Veronica, at nine, has "no idea" of Sally's last name. I watch the girl try to draw the maid. She reaches for a black crayon, sets it down, reaches for a brown one, starts using it—legs long, fairly wide, a suggestion of feet, then the mid-body, a massive protuberant stomach. Now the artist hesitates. She puts down her crayon. She scans the other crayons. She picks up the black one: no. She summons the blue one: no. She returns to the brown one, uses it to draw a second, smaller but not unsubstantial, flattened circle, and then draws two vertical lines, which she connects to a smaller, more conventional circle. That is to be all, I begin to realize, when the crayon box, each crayon carefully put back in its original place, is firmly pushed a foot or so across the table toward the other side. There she is, a maid—a featureless face, a thick neck, no arms, a droopy, heavy body, with strong limbs to bear it. I see Veronica's unease. She tells me she is "no artist" (she tells me her mother is one, an "amateur painter"). She also tells me she'll have to look more closely at Sally and then try again one day to draw her. I nod and say, in response, without words, "not a bad idea"—and suddenly, out of nowhere, it seems, we hear steps, followed in seconds by the sight of a tray, with iced tea, milk, cookies. "Great," says Veronica, and again I nod, now to the human being who has prepared the tray and carried it to us.

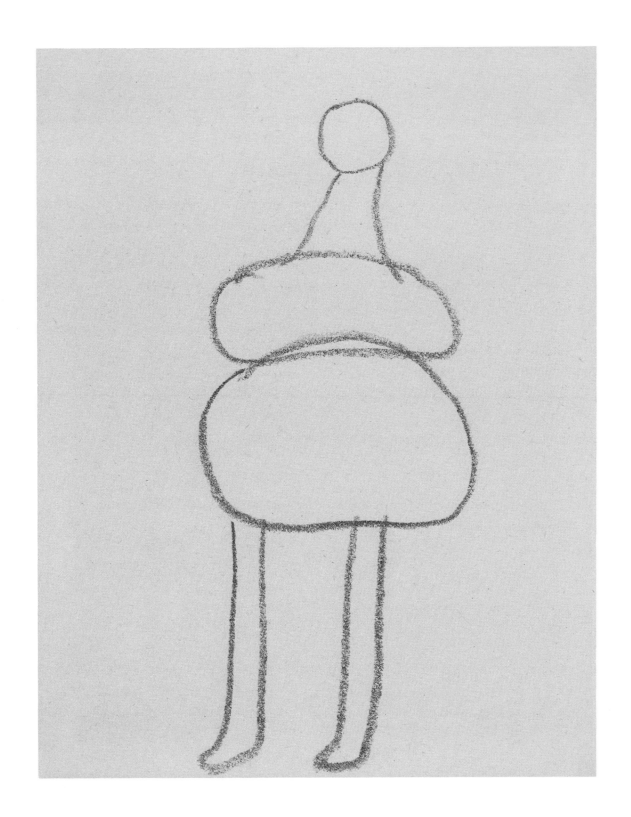

In Chattanooga, Joy Marie, only a month beyond her tenth birthday, has a wonderful time rendering a well-known biblical image, and does so to her own quite apparent amusement, though only gradually, to ours. My son Bob and I are not sure, at first, what she is doing. She works hard but says nothing; and we are doing our own work, reading notes we'd taken during an earlier drawing session with a group of children. At one point I notice the girl making letters—as in a cartoon, with words encircled and connected to the speaker. Who is this, and what has the picture got to do with the Bible? we wonder. We are puzzled when the drawing is handed us, and remain so, until the artist, taking pity, explains with two words: "Lot's wife." I am not able to move from that remark to a clear comprehension of what is there before me on paper. But Bob instantly gets the point, appreciates the wonderful, imaginative subtlety of the artist, her leap from ancient Israel to today's world of everyday objects: Lot's wife has the face and torso of a salt shaker, crying lest that be her final, irrevocable fate, her arms and legs, presumably, soon to be lost while the city burns—the price of looking back. The girl smiles twice, I think: once with satisfaction at her metaphoric leap as an artist and once at the slowness of the man to see and understand—though his son was not only quick to understand but quick to be the tactful interpreter.

At nine, among the Hopis, Miriam lets herself dream of the spirits who live on the mesa, or higher up, and who watch the world below, jumping, perhaps, from cloud to cloud. The sun enthralls her with its enormous power, its inscrutability. The sun has things to tell—and nature hears, then flowers. But the sun can kill, she well knows. On the other hand, deep within the world, deep down below the earth's surface, are wells of strength, which in their darkest, unseen presence can wage a great, successful struggle. "Even in the desert, there is life," Miriam reminds herself, and if the sun became too provocatively conquering, "something would happen": the wells would, finally, reveal their hidden authority. She often articulates this dialectic—warmth over the land, but a coolness deep within that is saving. She mentions hills and valleys, the ups and downs of a terrain, a people's "way." That last word means so much to her: "We have to keep our way." I ask about that, and she draws it—the sun-suffused sky, the adobe houses, the hill sloping toward the valley, the scattered green of desert vegetation, a tree's trunk, and beside it, right below it, given equal significance, a rock where she often sits and watches the world, a rock that she in her mind turns into (magnifies into) a chair. A vision of land sparsely settled, drenched in light, barely holding on, yet tested by centuries, proven thereby unconquerable.

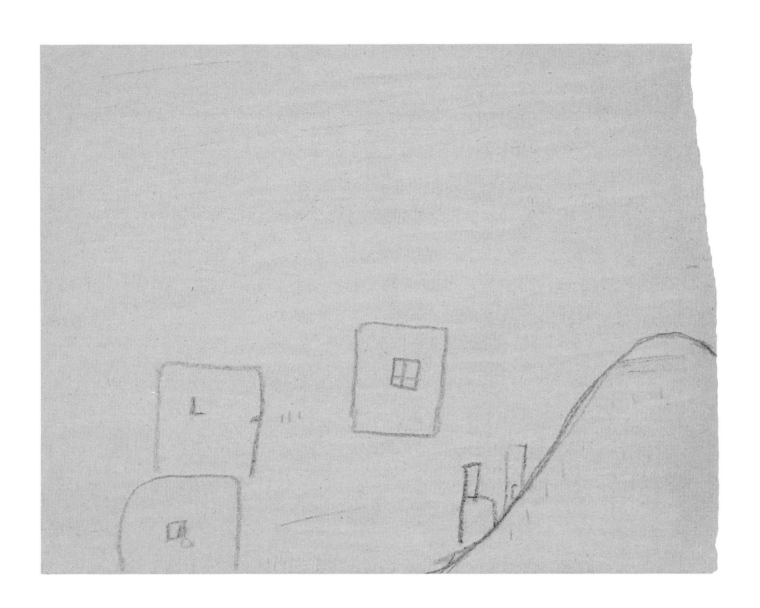

In Uppsala, Sweden, a nine-year-old girl, Johanna, is talking with my son Bob about "heroes." Her sense is that "the real ones" aren't "people," but rather "creatures of nature." Bob asks her for examples, and she is surprisingly unforthcoming. She scratches her head. She stares through the window at a nearby playing field, then looks away with an expression of displeasure: she has seen more of those human heroes, the strong and much admired athletes whom she wants to shun. Johanna fidgets, doodles a bit with a pencil, then draws a bird. She emphasizes its beak, and eye, and feet: "A bird is brave. She flies high, and she's not afraid of the wind, and she doesn't bother anyone, or try to be stronger and better! She's just herself!"

A child's avowal of modesty as a virtue—a pleasing, fragile beauty that captures her admiration, enables her to express a misgiving or two, indirectly, with respect to her quite assertive and successful parents (both of whom are college professors) and many of her friends, who are "tough," she has declared, by which she means "they want to be on top at school." She turns away from such ambitions, extols a different kind of lofty aspiration: to ascend effortlessly, to be unself-consciously lovely, to exist apart from all those whom she once, derisively, called "them," her ever so bright and talkative classmates. Instead, Johanna chooses another kind of heroism: she tries to escape the flesh to another order of being.